HARD WORK
IS NOT ENOUGH

HARD WORK IS NOT ENOUGH

THE SURPRISING TRUTH ABOUT
BEING BELIEVABLE AT WORK

JEFF SHANNON

NEW DEGREE PRESS

HARD WORK IS NOT ENOUGH
The Surprising Truth about Being Believable At Work

ISBN   978-1-63676-746-8   *Paperback*
        978-1-63730-489-1   *Kindle Ebook*
        978-1-63730-490-7   *Ebook*

To Mallory.

You are the best day of my life.

Contents

——

"There is more in us than we know. If we can be made to see it, perhaps, for the rest of our lives we will be unwilling to setting for less."

—KURT HAHN

Introduction

———

"You're doing it all wrong," said the guy in the swim lane next to me at my local college pool. I was learning to swim so I could compete in a triathlon the following month. It would be my first triathlon race, and it would begin with a five-hundred-meter swim in a murky lake with two hundred other competitors. I was anxious about the swim to start with, and the more I practiced, the worse I felt.

This swim practice looked a lot like the previous sessions. I would thrash through the water powered by sheer determination and stop at the other wall to catch my breath. Unfortunately, there would be no walls or other places to rest in the middle of the lake during the race.

"You training for a triathlon?" said the guy in the swim cap who was shark-like in the water.

"Yeah, how did you know?"

"You are swimming like a runner," he said with a smirk, like he'd seen dozens of guys just like me try to learn to swim before their first triathlon.

He continued, "Swimming isn't running. You can't muscle your way through water as you do on land. Water is eight hundred times denser than air. The harder you push against it, the harder it's going to push back. You need to change your whole approach."

From there, he taught me techniques that turned everything I believed about swimming on its head. Instead of pulling hard with my arms, I used my arms to point to the end of the pool. Rather than kicking hard and splashing, I would kick just enough to turn onto my side. Instead of holding my breath, I would breathe on every stroke.

Almost immediately, I could make it down and back without taking a rest break. In a few weeks, I swam my first five hundred meters in the pool without stopping. A month later, I completed my first triathlon and my first open water swim.

Jim, the guy in the other lane, was a master swimmer and triathlete himself, and he taught me a valuable lesson: "Hard work is not enough." It would change how I understand what it takes to succeed in the pool and in my career because it helped me realize the well-intended advice I received from my parents, teachers, and first managers was only part of the formula for success.

~~~~~

What advice did you receive when you started your career? What did people tell you to do to stand out from the crowd? Perhaps it was your parents or an early mentor who wanted to help you get off to a strong start and make a good impression with your new boss.

If you're like most professionals, someone told you how to get ahead was to become an expert in your field and work harder than everyone else. With the simple recipe in hand, you were ready to take on adulthood. If you committed fully to the strategy, you more than likely have experienced a significant amount of professional success.

If it's not broken, why fix it?

The problem is that it is broken. Sure, you are on the cusp of or settled into middle management. You're paid well. You have a lot of responsibility. Maybe you even lead a team. Heck, people probably look up to you! But are you satisfied? Are you fulfilled by the work you do? Is this where you see yourself in five, ten, or fifteen years from now?

Look around. See all those hardworking folks who seem to be lifers in their current role? Good people, no doubt. But do you want to stay with this group the rest of your working days, or do you aspire to achieve a different level of success?

Odds are at a certain point in your career, you will hit a career plateau. You know you're there when no matter what you seem to do, you no longer feel like you're moving forward.

You feel stuck, bored, or are struggling to find fulfillment. You're not alone.

According to a *Gallup* study on the quality of work, 33 percent of workers who claim to be in a "good job" are looking for new work. Think about it, one in three people are in what they describe as a good job, yet they are actively looking for a different position or to work somewhere else. We're not talking about advancement. It is important, but it's not as crucial as doing fulfilling work and making a material contribution.

Over a forty-plus year career, it seems logical you're going to reach one, two, or three plateaus in your life. Work that once challenged you is no longer fulfilling. You want to be trusted with greater responsibility. You want to contribute at a higher level. You want to leave a legacy of results.

It's not about credit, recognition, or pats on the back. It's not about getting something for nothing because you're willing to earn it. You want to be influential. Not in the sleazy, selfish way, but rather in the "Let me leave this place, this work, and the people I work with better than I found them" way.

You're at an inflection point. You face a choice about what you do and how you will do it.

You can use this moment to double down on the "expert and hard work" strategy by continuing to sharpen your hard skills and work twice as much you do today.

Or

You can recognize the "expert and hard work" strategy worked to get you where you are today, but it won't serve you for where you want to go tomorrow.

~~~~~

I found myself at one of these inflection points about eight years into my career. I loved the company, my work, and my colleagues, but I questioned the value I could create. I had moments here and there to influence a decision, but rarely were they of significant consequence. I was comfortable speaking up in meetings, but I didn't feel what I said carried much weight with the senior leaders.

During my annual talent review meeting with my manager, I was confident in my hard-earned expertise and stellar performance record. So, I was shocked to learn I was not in the top box on the talent rating and was considered "unpromotable" beyond the next level. When pressed, my manager said the organizational leaders felt I didn't get it, was too in the weeds, and couldn't see the bigger picture.

I vowed to double my efforts and prove to everyone I was promotable. I worked harder and longer than those around me. I took on more responsibility. I carried the load to prove I could do everything all by myself. I took the "expert and hard work" strategy as far as it could go, and it was right back where I started. Except for this time, I was burned out and even more frustrated.

Nothing changed for me until I learned hard work is not enough to succeed, not in the pool and not in my career.

In the pool, a chance encounter with Jim taught me what swimming expert Terry Laughlin teaches all his students, which is "water resistance (drag) is the largest factor limiting how far or fast we swim." This simple idea, which was previously invisible to me, required me to adapt my approach to the aquatic environment. When I shifted my focus on becoming more streamlined in the water rather than kicking and pulling my way through it, I experienced a dramatic improvement in my performance.

The experience in the pool made me ask myself, "What had changed in my work environment and was invisible to me?" When I looked around the office, nearly every colleague at my career level was an expert at something, and each one of them was working their tails off. However, few carried much influence with senior leaders. Most were trusted to do the work but not charged with decisions that would shape the company. It was then I realized expertise and work ethic was a great way to approach your first professional job. However, being known for dependability wouldn't be enough to have the impact I aspired to over my entire career.

Steve Kane, CFO of Airlite Plastics, explained it to me like this: "There is a benefit to learning one discipline well. You must have the hard skills, but many people can build a nice model, reconcile an account, or put together a report. It's not a differentiated skill beyond a certain level. So, you have to have soft skills, too." He's making a distinction between the learned technical skills and the social skills required to be successful at work. Best-selling author Simon Sinek reframes it as hard skills and human skills. "Hard skills are the skills you need to do your job and human skills are the skills you need to be a better human being. It's the human skills that make you a better leader."

Expectations change when you move from individual contributor to manager and from manager to leader. So, I needed to adapt my approach to those changing expectations. If I wanted to do meaningful work and influence my colleagues and the company, I would have to change how I behaved, thought, and led others.

As soon as I did, my career changed dramatically. I was promoted and then promoted again, and then asked to lead a business, and then asked to lead a a bigger business. Five years after that day in the pool, I was the Director of a business worth $1 billion in retail sales. Five years after that, I cofounded Bravium, a boutique facilitation and executive coaching firm, where I help people be more strategic, innovative, and effective leaders.

THE PROMISE

I have spent thousands of hours observing leaders in strategy offsite meetings, leadership development programs, and one-on-one coaching sessions. In that time, I have witnessed countless functional experts and leaders who are more than competent in their domain fail to influence others. They invested thousands of hours gaining the hard skills and expertise, yet midway through their careers nobody listens to them.

This book is about influence, but it's unlike other books about influence you've read before. That's because genuine influence is more than brain hacks, having more executive presences (whatever that means), or projecting a strong personal brand. It's about working on yourself rather than working on what others think of you.

Dependable   ## Believable

Someone known for their functional expertise and work ethic

$\neq$

Someone known for their ability to influence others with their behaviors, thinking and leadership

In the first few chapters, I will set the stage with a framework for influencing others and make a case for adopting new behaviors to increase your believability.

I will then synthesize years of leading businesses and helping companies build strategy into principles and frameworks to help you think and act more strategically.

Finally, I will provide you proven tools and a powerful mindset shift to help you make decisions and avoid common manager mistakes.

By the end, I hope you see how learning to influence others is really about transforming how you see yourself. Influence, I've grown to understand, is not a list of skills designed to get people to listen to you, take your advice, or position yourself.

Instead, genuine influence starts with transforming who you are and how you show up in the world.

CHAPTER 1

Go Further Upstream

—

You hear a knock at your door. It's 9:00 a.m. and you aren't expecting anyone. However, a man you don't recognize is at your door. Could this be one of those fast-talking guys who want to sell you something? Do they work for one of the political parties or religious groups going door to door? Why are they here so late? Will you have to wait for the perfect time to interrupt their speech to tell them you're not interested?

The amygdala is the almond-shaped part in the medial temporal lobe of the brain. It enables you to feel certain emotions and to perceive them in other people. It seems to modulate our reactions to events and stimuli like eating, drinking, sex, and addictive drugs and is considered an essential part of our threat detection systems.

When you open the door, your body is sending around eleven million bits of information to your brain, and your amygdala plays a role in processing the information. It is always on and always processing information about your environment. For example, one of the questions it asks is, are they a friend or a foe? In other words, can I trust this person?

~~~~~

"We need more trust," says Barb to a room of thirty-five people who work together to put on the College World Series. Barb is a participant in a team alignment workshop I'm leading for the NCAA, and she is summarizing her small group assessment of why the team feels so much friction. The workshop was designed to help three different organizations work better together in producing one of the most exciting two weeks of sports that Omaha, Nebraska, has to offer. The CWS, as fans know it, is the men's Division I college baseball championship and has been in Omaha for the past seventy years. This event attracts 332,000 attendees and generates an estimated $74 million in just a couple of weeks.

According to the global survey of approximately 9,800 full-time workers on trust conducted by EY, Barb is not alone in her view. Only 49 percent of full-time workers responded they had "a great deal of trust" in those working above and alongside them. This means the other half of the survey respondents feel they don't have a great deal of trust! "We need more trust" is also one of the most common refrains I hear from teams looking to operate at a higher level.

Working within an environment of trust can be a compelling experience. For example, Steve Booker, now president and CEO of SK Food Group, described a moment for me when the frozen foods business he led faced extraordinary cost inflation and profitability challenges. When asked how he overcame the obstacles in an interview, he said, "None of us within our team claimed to have all the answers. Instead, we recognized every one of us had a different view of the field we needed to understand. We created a culture where each team member felt free to share their view and related opinions. This enabled us to more accurately define our current reality and develop more effective action plans." He attributed the team's success to a feeling of trust among the team members that encouraged them to speak up, challenge each other, and act decisively.

In his book *Herding Tigers*, Todd Henry describes the feeling of trust well when he writes, "Trust is not like a bank account where you can make deposits and withdrawals. It's like a water balloon; one puncture, and you lose it everywhere." Almost everyone understands how important trust is to a relationship and to working on a team. Still, when pressed, most people have difficulty describing trust or knowing how to create it when it's lacking.

The Oxford English Dictionary defines trust as a "firm belief in the reliability, trust, ability, or strength of someone or something." The most important word is "belief," defined as something one accepts as true or real, a firmly held opinion or conviction. When someone says "we need more trust," what they mean is they want to believe in their colleagues' ability to do the work and have their backs. Steve's team believed in each other enough to share different perspectives, even competing views, when working together to overcome enormous obstacles.

Steve's team trusted each other, but that trust was a vehicle to something even more important: results. That year, Steve's team delivered record profitability despite an environment of unprecedented inflation. At the company's annual awards event, the team was recognized for their extraordinary results with the Brand Team of the Year, Innovators of the Year, and Culture Creators of the Year awards.

~~~~~

Trust is an essential ingredient for any working relationship. If you were baking a cake, trust is like flour; it's indispensable. Try and offer someone a cup of flour to eat at your next party and see how many takers you get. Flour needs to be combined with eggs, sugar, butter, and baking soda before it's cake batter. Even then, it still needs to be baked and frosted before someone can enjoy it. In other words, the flour needs to be activated before it turns into a cake.

If trust is the flour and results are the cake, then influence is the catalyst. Influence is the capacity to influence the character, development, or behavior of someone or something. Therefore, if you want to achieve results, especially with others, you will have to become more influential.

Humans have attempted to influence each other for thousands of years. The earliest recorded example is from forty-five thousand years ago when early Indonesians painted human-like figures hunting warty pigs and dwarf buffaloes on cave walls. I can only assume they were leaving a record of their accomplishments to influence the next generation. Perhaps they were saying "do it like this if you want to survive!"

The world has become more sophisticated since our days hunting with spears, which means it takes more than finger painting on cave walls to influence others. As a result, I've witnessed two approaches emerge when it comes to influencing. First, I introduced the "hard work and expertise" approach in the previous chapter and the method I tried with limited success. The second approach is the "personal branding" method. Unfortunately, neither of these approaches hit the sweet spot when it comes to genuine influence.

WHY THE HARD WORK AND EXPERTISE APPROACH DOESN'T WORK

In 1991, I had a huge crush, but it wasn't on a classmate. Instead, it was on Mrs. Troyer, my algebra teacher. I was so head over heels, I purposely earned detention to spend time in her classroom after school. (Oh, the logic of a fourteen-year-old boy!)

One of her lessons that has stuck with me to this day was a little game we played to maximize revenue dollars generated from selling pretend widgets by setting the optimum price. When we completed the exercise, she showed us revenue was a bell curve. The line went up as you raised the price, but it began to come back down again when the higher price reduced the total units sold. This paradox of the bell curve is something that has fascinated me ever since.

Before we get into the paradoxes of hard work and expertise, we need to talk about judgment. More specifically, we need to talk about other people's judgment of you. We know people shouldn't judge, but the fact is they do. Other people form opinions about you based on very little information, affecting your success at work. It's ugly, unfair, and can be hurtful, but it's a lot easier to accept it and devise a better strategy than hoping people won't judge you.

On the bell curve of hard work, let's call the x-axis *effort* and the y-axis *influence*. The far left of the curve represents what everyone wants to avoid, which is the perception of being lazy. You probably intuitively recognize you have little or no influence if others perceive you as lazy. If you increase your effort, you will see your degree of influence begin to rise and peak and begin to come back down. The reason for the peak and decline is because expectations (the z-access) are also increasing. What was once a differentiator is now expected. At a certain point, working too hard and too long begins to be perceived as someone who can't be strategic, can't prioritize, or is ineffective.

HARD WORK PARADOX

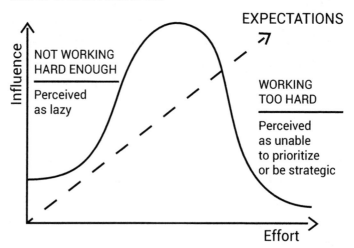

The same bell curve also applies to subject matter expertise. In the beginning, more expertise in a field differentiates you from your peers. Your early success raises expectations to new and higher levels. Here being an expert on a single topic leads people to perceive you as one-dimensional. They assume your depth makes it challenging for you to see the bigger picture or to connect the dots to the larger organization. The translation is you're so good at a narrow and deep topic, how could you possibly be good at context and strategy across other functions?

EXPERTISE PARADOX

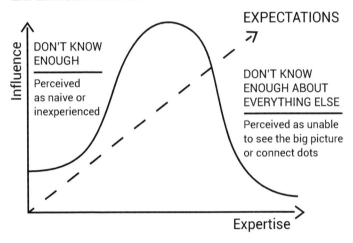

Are there exceptions to this rule? Yes! Some people who can overcome perception and bias. Hat's off to you if you are one of those lucky individuals. The thing about exceptions is they are rare, maybe one in a thousand. Are you going to bet your career on being the one in a thousand?

If yes, it's here where I wish you good luck and godspeed. However, if you're like me and didn't win the talent lottery, there is more to do to be more believable. Let's quickly explore why personal branding doesn't work before we get into my recommended approach.

WHY PERSONAL BRANDING DOESN'T WORK, EITHER

I'm often asked to lead training on personal branding or to coach someone on executive presence. Well-intended managers want me to help make their team members more influential. They describe their employees as hardworking and highly capable individual contributors and managers who struggle to present themselves and their ideas. They hope a workshop on personal branding will do the trick.

A quick Google search of "personal branding" results in thousands of articles and blog posts with titles like *How to build your personal brand without the cringe* or *3 Reasons Why You Should Cultivate a Kick-Ass Personal Brand*, encouraging readers to build their brand. Medium, a popular digital publishing platform, has an entire page dedicated to the topic of personal branding. What exactly is personal branding? According to Influencer MarketingHub, your personal brand is how you promote yourself. It is the unique combination of skills, experience, and personality you want the world to see.

Dwayne Johnson is an excellent example of a global personal brand. What you might not know is the Rock, as his WWE fans know him, has a team of people managing his image and deals to make him one of the world's highest-paid celebrities. Dany Garcia, CEO of TGC Management Group, a holding company that manages the personal brand for Dwayne Johnson, said in an interview with Kia Ryssdal, "There's nothing in his expressions...that don't relate to everything he does in a single day." What she means by *expressions* is the truck he drives, the sneakers he wears, and the tequila in his glass are all designed to influence his 212 million followers and make him the twenty-ninth highest-grossing actor of all time (over $12.2 billion worldwide). Again, it's modern-day product placement, but instead of Reese's Pieces in the movie ET, it's Dwayne Johnson with a video of himself working out in his line of Under Armour clothing.

How might personal branding help you gain more significant influence? In short, it doesn't. The personal branding approach tries to manage people's impression of you. It is exhausting to you and everyone else. There are just too many people and too many opinions to maintain.

I once worked for a manager who took this approach, and it was infuriating because you never knew which version of them would show up. They were utterly unpredictable because they always tried to read the situation with their manager and flip-flopped on decisions. Their north star was whatever led to the most favorable impression at the moment, rather than a set of core beliefs and principles. It left me questioning who I was dealing with at any given moment. In the end, it made it hard for me and others to trust this person.

THE RIVER OF INFLUENCE FRAMEWORK
It might be helpful to think of all of this as a river and the results you hope to achieve are way downstream. Let's

imagine you're paddling a canoe in a swift-flowing river. If you don't make decisions upstream, it will be too late. The river will carry you right into danger, and there's not much you can do about it.

For instance, suppose you needed to exit the river at a particular point. Otherwise, you would go over a four-foot waterfall two hundred yards downstream, destroying the canoe and likely drowning you and your daughter. This image flashed through my mind when my wife Jen nearly missed the last exit on the Niobrara River during a family trip in 2020. (Don't ask her about it; she not ready to laugh about it yet!)

THE RIVER TO INFLUENCE

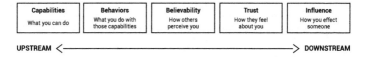

Capabilities	Behaviors	Believability	Trust	Influence
What you can do	What you do with those capabilities	How others perceive you	How they feel about you	How you effect someone

UPSTREAM <———————————————————————> DOWNSTREAM

The same holds for trust. Downstream from trust is influence and then results. Trying to solve the problem downstream with personal branding doesn't work because it is trying to manage other people's impressions, and that's too difficult control.

Working directly on trust may even be too late. When participants in my workshop say "we need more trust," they're assuming trust is something we can control or change in another person. It's much easier to think of trust as a feeling someone else holds about you and isn't something you can control. Releasing this notion frees you from worrying or trying to manage what other people think about you. Instead, you can focus squarely on how you behave, think, and lead others. To do that well, we need to go further upstream to believability.

For our purposes, believability is defined as credible or convincing. To be believable is a combination of capabilities and behaviors. Capabilities are what you can do. They include your technical abilities and your subject matter expertise. Behaviors are your actions and how you connect with other people. They include how you present yourself and your ideas.

Unfortunately, the world is full of technically competent people who have acquired a long list of degrees and certifications who have no influence whatsoever. Rare is the person whose technical competence outweighs their social incompetence. The same can be said for the person with excellent interpersonal skills but who doesn't know what they're talking about. They are likable, just not someone you want to take advice from when the stakes are high.

I am assuming you have already developed the capabilities needed to be successful, so the rest of this book will focus on behaviors to help you be more believable. We will start with understanding four critical principles of being believable.

FOUR PRINCIPLES OF BELIEVABILITY

BELIEVABILITY REQUIRES A RECORD OF RESULTS

LeBron James will go down as one of the greatest to ever play basketball. He is unquestionably a brand, and he is a proven entity. For example, suppose you hire James on your team.

You are almost sure to make it to the NBA Finals. As of 2020, James has led his team to the finals ten times out of sixteen seasons and walked away with four championships.

Achieving results is foundational to being believable. Without results, anything you do or say will be doubted by others. For example, each year when I worked in the food industry, I was responsible for one of the new hires who had just graduated with their MBA. They would come in with big ideas on what needed to change and how things could work better if we would listen to them. These were intelligent people, and some of the ideas were outstanding, but it didn't matter. They weren't believable because they hadn't generated any results beyond graduating school.

BELIEVABILITY BEGINS LOCALLY

You've probably never heard of Rick Barker. Reading his name, you might think he's the little brother of the famous game show host of *The Price is Right*, Bob Barker, but you couldn't be further from the truth. Rick Barker was the mastermind manager to launch the global juggernaut Taylor Swift. When she was sixteen years old and full of aspirations, he gave her some sage advice that helped her become the most influential person on Twitter in 2019 and sold over 37 million albums in the US over her career.

Early on, the aspiring young woman told Barker she wanted to be the biggest star in the world. According to the digital media group, One37pm, Barker told Swift she'd need to meet five hundred thousand people to achieve her goals. Swift described her fateful exchange with Barker as "He was the first one to ever say that to me, and it sunk in." Barker's strategy for Swift in his own words was this: "We can teach you how to sing, we can get you songs, and we can put you on tours. We can do a lot of different things for you, but we can't teach you to care."

Just imagine how much time and energy it took to attend enough post-concert meet-and-greets to connect with five hundred thousand people when you're a sixteen-year-old kid with dreams of being a star. Believability starts with a record of getting results and intentionally building relationships with people you work with most. Having a great resume or five thousand connections on LinkedIn doesn't amount to much if you can't get the people closest to you to back you or your work.

BELIEVABILITY IS PUTTING WE BEFORE ME

Think back to the someone at the door scenario I used to open this chapter. What is the question you are asking yourself as you open the door? If you're like me, the question running through your mind is, "Who is it and what do they want?"

It is safe to assume everyone you work with is subconsciously asking the same question of you! Think about it like this: everyone you encounter at work has an amygdala and is also bombarded by the eleven million bits of data per second. Every one of those bits is processed and analyzed for threats. For simplicity's sake, the answer falls into one of two concepts: Me or We.

Are your behaviors communicating you want to serve your own needs or serve other's needs? For example, when a colleague at work takes credit for a project, whose needs are they serving? To be more believable, you must make it clear you intend to create value for others every day with every interaction.

BELIEVABILITY IS SITUATIONAL

In 1993, I was an usher at the Q-cinema-9 movie theater. I wore faded black pants, a white shirt, and a little red bowtie. I loved movies and popcorn, so it was an excellent place for me to work, even if I was only earning $4.25 per hour. My job was to take out the trash and use that little powerless vacuum to clean the carpet. The film *Malice* came out that year, and I snuck into the back of the theater to hear the "God Complex" monologue repeatedly.

In the movie, Jeb Hill, a surgeon played by Alec Baldwin, is accused of having a God complex. With his shoulders back and relaxed in his chair and hand on his chin, Hill is unabashed in patronizing the opposition.

"Which makes me wonder if this…lawyer has any idea as to the kind of grades one has to receive in college to be accepted to a top medical school? Or if you have the vaguest clue about how talented someone must be to lead a surgical team? I have an M.D. from Harvard. I am board certified in cardiothoracic medicine and trauma surgery. I have been awarded citations from seven different medical boards in New England, and I am never, ever sick at sea."

The climax of Hill's sermon ends with advice for anyone looking for God on that particular night could find him in operating room number two, as he declares "I am God" and walks out of the room.

Your credentials or CV are not what makes you credible. You can spend your entire career building a long list of accomplishments and accolades to lose it instantly with destructive behaviors. That's what happens to Dr. Jeb Hill's credibility when he nearly kills patient Tracy Safian, played by Nicole Kidman.

After Hill leaves the room, Safian asks a simple question:

"Ask God how many shots of bourbon he had before he cut me open?"

Pow! Those years of dedication to his craft and the resulting awards and recognition come down to the one moment when he makes a severe error in judgment that nearly cost someone their life.

Believability is always situational. You can have it in certain circles and on certain subjects, but like Rory Vaden, the author of Take the Stairs, says about success, "it's never owned, it is rented, and the rent is due every day." Furthermore, believability is temporary, and if you neglect it, it will go away or become obsolete. Therefore, it must be cultivated every day with everyone you meet.

~~~~~

The ability to influence others is essential for generating significant results. It separates those who make a lasting impact on an organization and those who don't. Upstream from influence is the feeling of trust others must have about you before they allow you to influence them. Even further upstream from trust is believability, which combines your capabilities and behaviors and is where you should invest your effort.

The rest of this book will give you several ways to elevate your believability with others so you can be trusted, have influence, and achieve results. First, however, we will begin by looking at the three common behaviors that destroy the believability of otherwise talented people.

CHAPTER 2

Don't Give Away Your Power

———

"She just gave away her power," whispered a colleague as we sat together in the auditorium. An executive began her speech with "Good afternoon, my name is..." before she presented for the next fifteen minutes. It was a game a few of my closest work friends played to entertain ourselves during the long hours in meetings watching one disappointing presentation after another. The game's purpose was to entertain, but it also was our reminder of how important it was to be influential. It wasn't just what you could do but how you did it that mattered.

Any time I made the occasional misstep in presenting myself, ideas, or recommendations, I could count on a colleague sending me a text reading, "Dude! You just gave away your power!" These were the embarrassing words you never wanted to hear or read because if you did, you just failed to live up to the group's standards for believability.

The game was a friendly competition that shined a light on our bad habits to help each other live up to the standards. You could give away your power in any number of subtle ways, such as minor "ums" or "ahs" when presenting to a group, appearing disorganized or unprepared, and definitely being late to a meeting.

This silly little game taught me the significance of treating "the how" you do things as a craft of equal to "the what" you do because it helped me become more believable. Of course, each of us needed to behave in new ways to be more believable. Yet, it was more important to stop doing things that hurt our believability first.

~~~~~

If you've ever attended a team building workshop, then you are probably familiar with the Keep, Stop, Start exercise. It's an activity beloved by facilitators because it helps participants begin to discuss their team's most pressing behavioral issues. The activity includes posing three questions intended to open a productive dialogue among the participants. It begins with asking "What should the team keep doing?" followed by "What should the team stop doing?" and finally, "What should the team start doing?"

For example, the facilitator will ask the participants, "What should the team keep doing?" Then, each participant will write down a few ideas and share them with the group. It doesn't take very long to accumulate a bunch of post-it notes like "communicating" or "trusting each other" or "having each other's back."

What's most interesting to me, as the facilitator, is when the participants successfully answer the "keep doing question," they typically want to skip the middle "stop doing" question. Instead, they almost always want to move directly to answering the final "start doing" question. There seems to be more enthusiasm for identifying new behaviors rather than looking at old behaviors that may no longer serve the team. I suspect the participants feel there is less risk identifying new behaviors than admitting what they are doing today may be inadequate or ineffective.

It might be challenging to accept your current mindset and behaviors might hurt your believability despite your technical competence and work ethic. Like the participants who answer the "What should the team stop doing?" question head-on, it often provides the most meaningful insights. You can never grow if you don't take a hard look at your existing behaviors and attitudes that aren't serving you. Uncovering bad behaviors and stopping them can be equally as powerful as starting new and better behaviors. It can help you stop giving away your power and start making you more believable at work. So, before we go deeper into those believability eroding behaviors, let's take a momentary detour back to physics class.

~~~~~

You may recall the formula for measuring power is force times distance divided by time. (Don't worry, there won't be a test!) Imagine yourself pushing a stalled car off of the road. The force is how hard you have to push the vehicle. The distance is how far you have to push it. So it's safe to assume

Brian Shaw, four-time World's Strongest Man, is more powerful than you because he can push the same car the same distance much faster than you. I'm guessing, depending on the size of the car, Shaw could just pick it up and throw it out of the way!

The formula for measuring power in the work setting is similar, except instead of moving the car, you're moving people to act. Force is the effort you must exert to influence people with your actions, ideas, and words. Distance is how far you can move people, and time is how quickly you can move them. So, people with more power move more people further and faster than those who don't. Powerful people are believable and more influential. As a result, they can have a greater impact on an organization.

To understand giving away your power begins with an assumption that you have a certain amount of power to influence others within you. As introduced in the previous chapter, your functional expertise and work ethic can be multiplied by your behaviors to make you more or less believable. To give away your power is to consciously (or more likely unconsciously) do or say things that make you less believable to others.

An example is being overly efficient with people. You've been on the receiving end of this bad behavior if you've ever tried to talk to someone and they are looking at their phone or are trying to finish typing their email and listening to you simultaneously. The other person is putting their work first and making you feel insignificant in the process. We shouldn't behave in this way, yet we've all done it before. The risk is the more you repeat these behaviors, the more part of you they become.

~~~~~

For the sake of simplicity, let's assume you are expert enough and hardworking enough compared to your peers. (If not, then you should fill in those gaps first.) We can then split "how you do things" into two groups. First, attract behaviors that increase your believability, and second, repel behaviors that decrease your believability.

Attractive behaviors are those self-mastery, strategic, and relationship skills that pull people and opportunities to you. (This is not to be confused with attractive or physical looks) These are the behaviors, when combined with your capabilities, that make you more believable at work.

On the other hand, repellant behaviors are those habits and routines that push people and opportunities away from you. The result of this looks like not being selected to work on projects, bosses who don't trust your work, or being passed over for new roles in your organization. In other words, behaving in ways that repel people from you erodes your believability.

In his book the *Unbeatable Mind*, former Navy SEAL Commander and founder of SEALFIT Mark Divine recounts an old parable often attributed to the Cherokee tribe, but its origins are debated. The story is about an old Cherokee man teaching his grandson about life.

"I have a fight going on in me," the old man said. "It's taking place between two wolves. One is evil— he is anger, envy, sorrow, regret, greed, arrogance, self-pity, guilt, resentment, inferiority, lies, false pride, superiority, and ego."

The grandfather looked at the grandson and went on. "The other is good—he is joy, peace, love, hope, serenity, humility, kindness, benevolence, empathy, generosity, truth, compassion, and faith. The same fight is going on inside you and every other person, too."

The grandson took a moment to reflect on this. At last, he looked up at his grandfather and asked, "Which wolf will win?"

The old Cherokee gave a simple reply. "The one you feed."

It's not just folklore; there is scientific theory to support the parable. In 1949, psychology professor Donald Olding Hebb in his book *The Organization of Behavior* put forward a theory of neuroplasticity that can be summed up as "neurons wire together if they fire together." Learning and growth take place in the brain the more you do something. You've experienced this in nearly all aspects of your life, including learning to walk, doing multiplication, or throwing a ball. The more you do the activity, the more neurons will fire together, and the better and more natural the activity or thinking becomes for you.

This phenomenon works the other way, too. The less you do something, the weaker the connections become. Phone numbers can provide a great case study. How many phone numbers do you know by heart? If you're like most people (over the age of thirty), it's not as many as it used to be.

A global study conducted by Kaspersky Lab to analyze how digital devices and the internet affect the way people recall and use information today found "half of surveyed adult Europeans could not recall their children's or office phone numbers without looking into their mobile phones. Around a third were not able to remember their partner's number."

When we don't practice something, it fades away, which means we need to be mindful of the behaviors we practice; do more of those that serve us best and let go of those that take us on a downward spiral.

THE DOWNWARD SPIRAL OF BELIEVABILITY

Hundreds of behaviors could exist which might hurt your believability. Lying, cheating, and stealing are a few obvious ones you probably learned to avoid from family or teachers when you were a kid. Others are equally damaging but are more subtle, so they show up with regularity in the workplace. Three of the worst seem to be least noticeable by the person who exhibits the behaviors.

DOWNWARD SPIRAL OF BELIEVABILITY

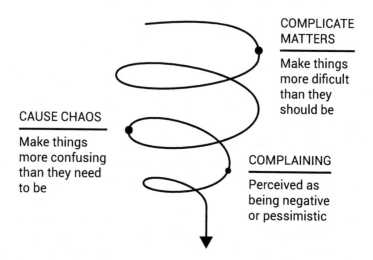

COMPLICATE MATTERS

Make things more dificult than they should be

CAUSE CHAOS

Make things more confusing than they need to be

COMPLAINING

Perceived as being negative or pessimistic

I've chosen to explain these as caricatures because I want you to experience the frustration of working with them can cause. As you read them, try to think about if they remind you of anyone you've ever worked with before. Ask yourself, is this person believable?

Following the brief stories, I will explain why the behaviors are so detrimental. I will then help you identify if you exhibit the behaviors unknowingly. Finally, I'll offer some suggestions for what you should do instead.

The first example describes a technical expert who struggles to build social capital. As a result, he has little influence beyond his functional domain, not because of technical skills but because of the rigidity of his attitudes and behaviors.

COMPLICATOR KARL

Karl loves his job and the company. He follows the rules and the chain of command. He's dependable and so consistent you can nearly predict his response to everything. Which means, you also know what to expect any time he's involved in a project or a task—more friction. Karl is so precise he can be insufferable at times. He is so detailed he loses sight of what you're trying to accomplish or why. He seems to have endless questions and a habit of making things more complicated than they need to be. He has trouble distinguishing between what does and doesn't matter; to Karl, everything matters. You like Karl, but you avoid working with him whenever you can because of the friction and extra work he creates.

"You are either a complexifier and simplifier," said my manager Barry Gisser, and he advised "you want to become a simplifier." In the example above, Karl gives away his power (and is less believable) because he has built a reputation for making things more complicated when he's involved. It repels people from wanting to work with him.

Becoming more believable requires you to maximize your capabilities with behaviors that reduce friction instead of creating it unnecessarily. So how do you know if you are a simplifier or complexifier? It isn't very scientific, but read the room. How people react to your ideas, questions, and processes can be great feedback on how you make them feel. For example, do people get frustrated or exhausted around you or avoid you altogether? Do people ask for your help and tell you how you make things so much easier for them? People's actions will tell you a lot more about how they feel about working with you than a 360-feedback survey ever could.

Here are three ways to avoid being a complexifier:

1. Think about the real objective or challenge to overcome behind the request or project. Then ask yourself what the most straightforward path to achieving the objective is. This approach is inspired by Occam's razor, a mental model named after William of Ockham, a fourteenth century friar, philosopher, and theologian renowned for his ability to deduce concepts to their simplest form. The thinking can be summarized as follows, "Among competing hypotheses, the one with the fewest assumptions should be selected." Choose the simplest solution first.

2. Separate the essential from the trivial by listing out the available facts and ranking them based on how important they are to the decision or activity. Cut the list in half and proceed knowing you are using the most relevant information and leave the noise behind.

3. Reduce everything to three to five steps maximum. When you're trying to explain something to others, remember they are less familiar with the subject than you. If you give them too much information, they will quickly be overwhelmed and lose confidence in you because it feels too complicated. Keeping the process at three to five steps or phases makes anything look approachable, doable, and communicates you understand the problem.

~~~~~

The following example of giving away your power is paradoxical because the person is already responsible for several projects and teams. However, this person is leaving some of their believability on the table. To borrow a metaphor from renowned physical therapist and best-selling author Kelly Starrett when he describes ignoring a shoulder problem, it's "like driving a Ferrari with the parking brake on. It's still a Ferrari, but it's not performing as it should." Even when you have a big title and responsibility, you're not operating at your potential when you do things to hurt your believability.

CHAOS CINDY

Cindy is a highly talented, intelligent leader and is responsible for several active projects and teams. She has an uncanny ability to identify problems and has solutions at the ready. However, the word is she's hard to work for because she can be unpredictable. She has so much on her plate and is moving so quickly she leaves people on her team confused and frustrated. She spends most of her time in meetings with the execs, which means she often swoops in, changes direction, and swoops back out again before answering any questions. Cindy has an opening on her team that would be perfect for you, and she's approached you about the opportunity. Unfortunately, she didn't have time to explain it, which leaves you doubting if you could weather the storm.

Nothing ruins the momentum and cohesion of a team like stress caused by confusion and uncertainty. For instance, British researchers published a study in *Nature Communications* that asked forty-five study participants to turn over digital rocks on a computer. If the participants chose a rock with a virtual snake under it, they received a painful electric shock. The researchers found knowing there was a 50 percent chance of receiving a shock was more stressful for the participants than when they knew they would be shocked every time.

The higher uncertainty of being shocked or not was more stressful than knowing for sure they would be shocked regardless of their choice. Believable people understand when people are stressed out by uncertainty or ambiguity their performance worsens. Therefore, they work to reduce uncertainty with their actions and words.

To measure if you are creating uncertainty at work, you need to look inward. Think about the last couple of weeks and ask yourself if things have felt messy, frustrating, and stressful. If you felt that way, so did everyone around you. Some it is probably out of your control, but some of it isn't. So do a quick review and capture in a journal what role you played in adding uncertainty to the situation. From there, you're ready to grow from the experience.

Here are three ways to reducing uncertainty for others:

1. Most managers are flying by the seat of their pants, which shows in their thinking quality. To combat this, don't trust your first draft of any plan. It may be clear to you in your mind, but I promise you, others don't see it so clearly. Taking five to ten minutes to gather your thoughts on a piece of paper will dramatically improve the clarity

and completeness of your ideas, directions, and requests to your team.

2. Build routines and communicate them to the team. You may be unable to predict the specific problems or adversity your team will face on a project, yet you can expect there will be some wrench in your plan. Build in some checkpoints or guardrails into the plan, so everyone knows when and how you will make adjustments. Use simple statements like, "If this happens, we will do this instead." Too many plans assume everything will go smoothly, which is the exception and not the rule.

3. Aim for effectiveness over efficiency. The Hall of Fame basketball coach John Wooden wisely asked, "If you don't have time to do it right, when will you have time to do it over?" One of the fastest ways to reduce uncertainty is to over-invest in people and projects upfront. Take whatever time you spend helping people understand the plan and double it, then measure if you get fewer questions and less rework than usual. As a facilitator, I am conscientious about giving people basic instructions to complete an activity in a workshop. I give them one or two simple steps to complete, repeat it, ask someone to explain the instructions in their own words, and finish by asking if they have any questions. Do you know what happens next? As I walk around the room, small groups will ask me, "So what are we supposed to do in this activity?" Even when they get it, they don't get it. Like a remodeling project, plan on spending twice as much time as you predicted, and you will still only be halfway.

~~~~~

The final example for giving away your power may be the most insidious because it's so common you may hardly notice you do it, and it takes constant vigilance to avoid sliding back into the habit.

COMPLAINING CHARLES

Charles is a hard worker and has strong opinions about what's not working around here. The funny thing is he's not wrong—things could be a lot better, but his constant negativity brings everybody down. It's as if we can't do anything right and nothing is working, which is unfair and untrue. You know there are many positives, but it is just hard to see them when you're around Charles. The last time you went to lunch with him, you listened to him go on and on about how this doesn't work, or those people are idiots. You spent the rest of the day in a total funk and went home in a bad mood. It's gotten so bad lately, you made a promise to yourself to avoid him tomorrow.

Expressing dissatisfaction comes in many forms, like verbalizing your frustration or annoyance through protesting, whining, or lamenting. It can also come in the form of eye-rolling, moaning, grumbling, or groaning when something or someone doesn't meet your standards or expectations, and it can be so natural you don't even notice it. Will Bowen, the best-selling author and creator of the Complaint Free challenge, says, "Complaining is like bad breath. You notice when it comes out of someone else's mouth, but not so much when it comes out of your own." Complaining and negativity is a powerful force. It spreads, and worst of all, it's usually invisible to the person doing it.

I conducted a poll on LinkedIn where I asked my network, "Who would you rather work with daily, someone who is an expert who complains, or a non-expert who never complains?" Sixty-nine percent of respondents said they would rather work with a non-expert who never complains. How should we interpret this survey? Two-thirds of people are so turned off by complaining they would instead work with someone less competent in their role.

Jeff Shannon
Strategist | Facilitator | Coach | Author
3mo ·

Want to help me with research for my book Hard Work Is Not Enough? Take the poll:

Who would you rather work with daily? Someone who is an:
You can see how people vote. **Learn more**

Expert who complains	33%
Non-expert who never complains	67%

105 votes · Poll closed

3 · 12 comments

Here are three ways to avoid complaining and negativity:

1. Stop saying negative things out loud. In an interview with Cheddar Shakers, Trevor Moawad explains learning how to be less negative is more powerful than being more positive. Moawad is a renowned mental conditioning expert and strategic advisor to some of the world's most elite

performers and teams. He suggests we "be very mindful of what you say out loud; it's ten times more powerful than when you think it, and if it's negative, it's a multiple of four to seven times." Mowad is saying something we know intuitively: negativity spoke out loud is forty to seventy times more powerful than if not said at all. Of course, negative things happen to us all, but how we talk about those things makes a difference in our believability.

2. Surround yourself with the right people. Complaining at the proverbial water cooler can be satisfying for sure, but it's a risky move if you want to be more believable at work. When I asked Jennifer Baker, senior director at Supportworks, what is the one bit of advice she would give to any new employee, she said, "I've seen many employees who are negatively impacted by being in a work friend group that focuses on the problems at work. Every organization has challenges, but allowing yourself to be caught in a group that focuses on the negatives can impact both your perception of the organization and the organization's perception of you. It's like the old saying—who you spend time with is who you become." Watch who you're spending time with at work. If you find yourself having to defend their cynicism to others by saying, "you just have to get to know them better," it may be time to move on.

3. Let go of your expectations. In his TEDx talk, Shaolin Master Shi Heng Yi describes Bhuhda's Five Hindrances to achieving clarity. Master Shi uses the metaphor of climbing a mountain and how the five hindrances will create obstacles to keep you from reaching the top. For example, the second hindrance is VYAPADA or ill will. He describes it as "an aversion or rejection, or simply a dislike, against either an object or situation or can be

even a person." His metaphor describes work perfectly. You go to work with a set of expectations, but something impedes your progress, and you begin to complain, which then permits you to give up.

In his famous recording *The Strangest Secret in the World*, Earl Nightingale described the mind like a farmer's land: "The land doesn't care what seeds the farmer plants. It will return in just as much abundance, something healthy or something poisonous. It's up to the farmer to decide." So, likewise, it's up to you to determine what you plant in your mind and the mind of others. Do you want to be known as a person who complains about their circumstances or someone who does something about them? If you're going to be more believable, it's the latter.

~~~~~

Still wondering why "Hello, my name is..." should never be a presentation starter? It's because this is how a child might give their very first presentation in elementary school. You're a confident and believable adult who knows their stuff inside and out. A better way to launch into a presentation is "Hello, I'm...and I'm here to talk to you about..." It's a subtle cue to the audience that you are a confident, competent presenter, and once you try it on for yourself, it just feels better to say. This was a lesson we learned from Dave Koll, chief principle of FirstCaptivate, a training and development firm specializing in helping people be compelling and relevant leaders.

Becoming more believable at work requires you to adopt new behaviors that attract people and opportunities to you.

However, the priority should always be to avoid the attitudes and behaviors that repel people, and the best way to do that is not to give away your power. You have power over your habits because how you spend your energy tells your brain what is most important and what it should make easier for you by building strong synapsis. Once you can do it consistently, you're ready to move on to the one behavior that can help you do everything else.

CHAPTER 3

Drink the Ants

———

When he was nineteen, Derek Neeley experienced something that changed his life forever. Derek described himself as a typical American kid who loved sports and playing video games. After his freshman year at BYU, he began preparing for a mission trip. He spent eight weeks learning to do the work, learning how to navigate, and studying Spanish. Derek was headed to Guatemala, and for the next two years he would spend eighteen hours a day traveling by foot to meet with local people.

It takes about twelve hours to travel from Salt Lake City to Guatemala. Derek had never been there before, so the trip itself was a significant experience. It was hot, and the culture was strikingly different than what he expected. Derek described the experience in an interview: "The minute you get onto the airplane, they start speaking a language, and you're like, 'Wait a second, I thought I was studying Spanish, but that is clearly not Spanish.'" Then, to make the experience more stressful, people were yelling at him in the customs line when he arrived in Guatemala. Despite all his Spanish training, he had no idea what they were saying.

In his white shirt and tie with two luggage pieces, Derek rode a bus crammed full of people over questionable roads for four hours to the coastal village where he would call home for the next two years. In all, Derek's journey by airplane, bus, and on foot lasted over eighteen arduous hours. When he finally arrived at his destination, it was a corrugated tin-roof shack with chickens in the courtyard and no warm water.

Instead of resting, Derek went straight to work by visiting a member of his local church congregation. He said the host "did the most basic thing they could do and gave me a ham sandwich with Kool-Aid for dinner." It was a simple plate with a sandwich covered in ants. He recounted for me what he was thinking at the moment and said, "They're just scurrying around everywhere! It's fine; I'm okay." He shook off the sandwich the best he could and took a bite.

Next, Derek looks into his drink and sees a dozen live ants swimming on top of the Kool-Aid. He looks around and realizes ants are everywhere—on the table, the floor, and in the food on the shelves. It was at that moment, after one of the most exhausting and disorienting days of his life, where Derek had an epiphany.

He looked down into the glass of Kool-Aid and thought to himself, "I can spend the next twenty-four months picking ants out of my drink or I can decide I'm going to take every experience as it comes." So, he picked up the glass and drank the entire thing in a single gulp. He told me it was important to him to "make sure every drop was gone, and every ant was down the hatch" to prove it "wasn't a big deal." He then smiled and thanked his host for their hospitality.

By choosing to adapt to the environment rather than resist, Derek embraced a philosophy that would pay dividends for him years later as a vice president at Danone and as a father. He and his children use the "drink the ants" mantra whenever they need to face something uncomfortable or deal with adversity. He summed it up by saying, "There are so many things you cannot control, and sometimes you have to drink the ants. It's okay. It's alright. It's not going to kill you."

In the previous chapter, I introduced the concept of behaviors that repel or attract people and opportunities to you. Like the Keep-Stop-Start game, I suggested you keep working hard and building your technical competence. Next, I outlined three behaviors you should "stop doing" because they can undermine your believability. Finally, we are ready to explore the behaviors you should "start doing" to grow your influence.

Derek's "drink the ants" story serves as a great jumping-off point to increase your believability. The first step is to look at your adaptability and ask yourself, could you drink the ants if necessary?

~~~~~

"You guys are pathetic! Make me sugar cookies!" shouted our coach through a megaphone. It's six o'clock in the morning, and I and fifty other want-to-be-warriors were on a beach near Carlsbad, California. We were trying to do push-ups and sit-ups in sync as a single unit before the coach gave up on us and yelled, "Sugar cookie!" So we ran down the beach into the fifty-five-degree ocean water and then returned to the beach to cover ourselves in sand. (I found sand in my eyes, nose, and ears days later!)

Next was the final evolution I had been dreading since before I boarded the plane for California, Surf Torture. Our coaches instructed us to sit arm-in-arm, fifty people strong, with our backs to the surf and endure the waves washing over us. With each passing wave, I would inevitably gulp down a mouthful of seawater. I was covered in sand and shivering in the chilly water while I tried to keep two people next to me from being swept out by the tide. As intended by the coaches, the thirty-minute exercise incited discomfort and fear for all the participants.

I've shared this story with lots of people, and I get one of three reactions:

1. I hate the cold! I could never do that!
2. That sounds horrible! Why would you pay to do that?
3. Whoa! That sounds awesome! Where do I sign up?

These three responses are an excellent metaphor for thinking about adaptability, or the quality of being able to adjust to new conditions. For example, instead of surf torture, let's assume it's a big project at work. You are a mid-level manager looking for volunteers to help you with the project. You are likely going to get one of three reactions:

1. Thanks, but no thanks. I'm swamped. Besides, it's not really in my job description.
2. That sounds like a big project, and I've got a lot going. What exactly would I have to do?
3. It sounds like a big project. How can I help?

We should assume all three responses came from people who were already busy at work, and this new project is not what they were planning on when they arrived at work today. From your project leader's perspective, which response comes from the most believable person? Which person gives you the greatest feeling of trust? Which would you likely consider most influential?

In chapter one, I mentioned people shouldn't judge us, but the fact is they do. So how might the manager judge the three people they invited onto the project differently? The first person will likely not be asked again. The second person is kind of agreeing to help but is doing so begrudgingly. The third person is willing to change their plans to lend a hand quickly. Give me three people of equal capabilities and work ethic, and I will always choose the most adaptable person first.

Based on their responses to opportunities, it becomes easy to classify people into three categories when it comes to adapting to change:

1. Fossilized—People who refuse to change no matter the circumstances. They expect their manager, the work, and the company to yield to their wants and needs without conceding their current position.
2. Resistors—People who resist change. They cling to what is comfortable and familiar; they long for how things used to be. Out of necessity, Resistors eventually change. Still, it's slow, and it's painful, especially when you're their manager.
3. Early Adopters—People who are better at quickly accepting change and proactively looking for opportunities.

You can be a functional expert and have a strong work ethic. Still, you won't be believable if you can't or are unwilling to change or update your thinking or methods with new information. You must be willing to adapt.

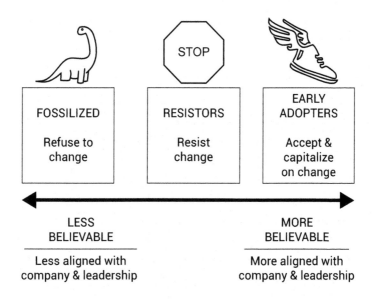

		EARLY ADOPTERS
FOSSILIZED	RESISTORS	
Refuse to change	Resist change	Accept & capitalize on change

LESS BELIEVABLE

MORE BELIEVABLE

Less aligned with company & leadership

More aligned with company & leadership

Being in the early adopter group of people who embrace change and adapt quickly is crucial because marketplaces and companies are changing swiftly. Career paths are changing, too. Long gone are the forty-year jobs and a pension. According to the Bureau of Labor Statistics, the average tenure with an employer for Americans over age twenty-five is 4.9 years, down 6 percent from 2010. I don't see that trend reversing anytime soon.

Businesses need to change if they want to survive. They have to update their operating systems, infrastructure, capitalization, innovation, and talent if they are going to compete and win in the marketplace. If they don't, they will be obsolete. Therefore, early adopters who can change at the company's pace have to be more valuable than those who cannot or who are unwilling to adapt. The challenge is recognizing the change as it's happening.

~~~~~

Think about the last time you rode in a car going seventy-five miles per hour, and comparing that to riding in a commercial airplane going 550 miles per hour; the sensation is the same. Once you reach your cruising speed, it doesn't feel like you're moving inside the cabin. Your eighty-to-one-hundred-year life relative to the history of human existence is similar. You may experience brief moments of acceleration and deceleration like graduations, weddings, or looking at pictures of your children when they were still little. Still, most of the time, you likely barely notice the time passing by, and it makes it easy to assume tomorrow will feel a lot like yesterday.

Yet change is ever-present, and Ray Kurzweil, author, inventor, and futurist, explains in his essay on the law of accelerating returns how change is also accelerating. According to Kurzweil, the first technologies like sharp edges, fire, and the wheel took tens of thousands of years to develop. Change was moving so slow people living in that era likely wouldn't notice anything different at the beginning or end of any given one-thousand-year period. However, Kurzweil says things begin to change around 1000 A.D. when progress began to accelerate, where it might only take one hundred years to notice technological advancements. He says, "In the nineteenth century, we saw more technological change than in the nine centuries preceding it. Then in the first twenty years of the twentieth century, we saw more advancement than in all of the nineteenth century."

Consider change was almost inconsequential for tens of thousands of years, then becomes noticeable over thousands of years, then hundreds of years, then just twenty years. For proof, think about your smartphone. Apple released the first iPhone on June 7, 2007. Before that, people just stared into their empty hands while walking around!

Kurzweil predicts, "The twenty-first century will see almost a thousand times greater technological change than its predecessor." If his prediction is correct, it will bring consequences we cannot yet imagine. Some people's lives and careers will be upended, and some will find ways to adapt and take advantage of the opportunity. Regardless of the environment, the tragedy, and the misfortune one faces, there is always the story of someone who faced dire circumstances and prevailed in the end. Someone always comes out better for the change. Shouldn't it be you?

Adaptability is as much of an attitude as it is a skill that can be learned. No matter your degree of adaptability, you must learn to adapt faster than you do today to be more believable at work. There are three steps you can take to being more adaptable.

1. Accept your new circumstances.
2. Unlearn what you believed to be true.
3. Prepare for the unexpected.

There isn't an exact recipe or set of tactics to follow to improve your adaptability. So, I will explain each strategy with a story to illustrate the point. Hopefully, you will aspire to be more adaptable and more believable at work.

ADAPTABILITY STEPS

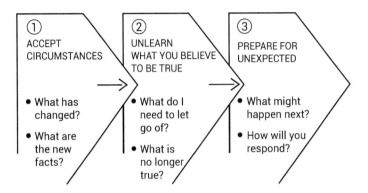

① ACCEPT CIRCUMSTANCES
- What has changed?
- What are the new facts?

② UNLEARN WHAT YOU BELIEVE TO BE TRUE
- What do I need to let go of?
- What is no longer true?

③ PREPARE FOR UNEXPECTED
- What might happen next?
- How will you respond?

ACCEPT YOUR NEW CIRCUMSTANCES

On the morning of July 31, 2008, my wife Jen and I learned our newborn baby boy had a genetic disorder called Down syndrome. It's a rare disorder, about 1 in 800. Still, at the same time, it's also one of the most common forms of intellectual disabilities. I didn't know much about Down syndrome, but I did know my life had profoundly changed from what I expected when we walked into the hospital the night before.

It was a rough few hours for Jen and me in the recovery room. We cried. We tried to come to grips with the situation. We cried some more. This was our first baby, and things were moving so fast during the delivery.

While the midwife and other nurse attended to Jen, I sensed something wasn't going as planned. So, I asked the nurse who was measuring and cleaning our son if everything was alright.

She didn't answer. I tried again.

"Hey, is everything normal?"

She wouldn't look at me.

She handed the baby to the midwife, who then passed the baby to Jen and said as plainly and compassionately as one could, "Congratulations on your son. He has Down syndrome. It's going to be alright."

I'm bringing this story up in a chapter on adaptability because it's my best "drink the ants" moment. The facts of the situation were Jen and I would walk out of the hospital with a new baby boy in two days. Later that afternoon, dozens of unaware family and friends would visit us, wanting to celebrate our first child.

We could resist the change thrust upon us, or we could accept it. We could let the fear of the unknown paralyze us, or we could get busy getting on with it. We could look backward and ask why, or we could look forward and ask how. We could think about challenges way down the road, or we could focus on what is next. We agreed we would share in the joy of having our first child and convey the "we got this" confidence we hoped to have when the dust settled.

Were we ready for this new responsibility? Not on your life! We weren't competent enough to be parents, let alone parents of a baby with special needs. We had no special skills. We had no unique character qualities that made us more qualified to care for someone with a disability than anyone else.

Two thousand years ago, Epictetus, the slave turned stoic philosopher, described how to deal with life's circumstances like this: "The chief task in life is simply this: to identify and separate matters so that I can say clearly to myself which are externals not under my control, and which have to do with the choices I actually control. Where then do I look for good and evil? Not to uncontrollable externals, but within myself to the choices that are my own."

Accepting your new circumstance is the first step to adaptability. It keeps you from clinging to the past or leaping ahead to the future and helps you be fully present and aware of the moment as it's happening. Acknowledging the discomfort gives you a degree of power so you can take the next step of unlearning what you believed to be true.

UNLEARN WHAT YOU BELIEVED TO BE TRUE

It lasted for just forty-seven seconds. Thus, Auguste and Louis Lumiere began the age of cinema with the first motion picture in history titled *La Sortie des Ouvriers de l'Usine Lumiére (Workers Leaving the Lumiére Factory)*. The year was 1895. The inventors from Lyon, France, drew acclaim and put their names down in history with their showing of the film on December 28, 1895 to an audience at the Grand Cafe on the boulevard des Capucines in Paris. Their invention was an eleven-pound, single-camera box with pins and claws moving celluloid film strips through the device at sixteen frames per second.

Within the year, the brothers used the cinematographer to film over forty moments of everyday life in France, including bustling city street scenes, the arrival of a train, and a person feeding a baby. It's at this point you expect the story to be about how Auguste and Louis Lumiere go on to create a cinema empire, but you would be dead wrong. Instead, the Lumieres stopped making films with their patented device. It's believed Louis Lumiere said it was "an invention without a future."

Andrew Davis, best-selling author and host of The Loyalty Loop, coined the term for how the two brilliant men, instead of building a movie monopoly, walked away from what today, in the United States, is a $703 billion industry. Davis calls it Lumiere's Law, and he describes it by stating, "The Lumiere brothers used their intimate knowledge of photography as a lens for understanding the potential of motion pictures." He says the Lumieres underestimated what was possible with their new invention because of what they already knew about photography. They failed to unlearn what they already knew about how to use a camera. As a result, the Lumieres couldn't see any possibilities beyond those they already accepted as true.

Lumiere's Law shows up anytime you make an assumption about the future based on what you already know about the past. It's when you assume the new leader of your team will operate the same way as the past leader. It happens when you utter the words "we tried that already" when someone throws out a solution. It reveals itself when you assume because your company is growing today it will keep growing tomorrow.

The lesson here is to not be a victim of Lumiere's Law by making the same mistake as Auguste and Louis did in 1895. Adapting to the new reality means unlearning what you know to be true as quickly as you can and updating your data with the current facts. Ask yourself what facts you are resisting today. What ideas and mental models do you need to let go of to get on with things?

I have a post-it note I wrote to myself when the COVID-19 pandemic struck to remind myself to let go of the prior paradigm of running a small business: "Assume this lasts forever, now what?" To be financially viable in 2020 required an entirely new set of attitudes and behaviors I previously hadn't considered. The unique circumstances required me to empty my cup.

> *Nan-in, a Japanese master during the Meiji era, received a university professor who came to inquire about Zen. Nan-in served tea. He poured his visitor's cup full and then kept on pouring. The professor watched the overflow until he could no longer restrain himself.*

> *"It is overfull. No more will go in!"*

> *"Like this cup," Nan-in said, "you are full of your own opinions and speculations. How can I show you Zen unless you first empty your cup?"*

When you can unlearn what you believed to be true, you open your mind to new information and data that can flow in like the tea to take its place. Accepting your circumstances and unlearning are reactive strategies to adapting to change. I will finish with a proactive approach called preparing for the unexpected.

PREPARE FOR THE UNEXPECTED

Justin Medeiros was running as fast as he could down a dusty fifty-five-degree dirt road. In front of him was Mat Fraser, the four-time Fittest Man on Earth. Both men ran nearly out of control as they allowed their bodies to descend a treacherous path through the hills of Aromas, California. It's day three of the 2020 CrossFit Games, and the top twenty fittest men and women from all over the world are looking to be crowned the Fittest on Earth.

Before this event, Dave Castro, the director and mastermind behind the games, spent an entire year devising the most comprehensive and grueling test of the human body and mind imaginable. All nineteen of the events, which include swimming, max front-squatting, legless rope climbs, and handstand push-ups, to name a few, are entirely top secret until right before the games. Castro had a sinister smile as he revealed the events that would push the athletes to the breaking point and beyond.

CrossFit, which has gyms worldwide, defines its programming as "constantly varied, high-intensity functional movements" that apply to athletes of every form. As a result, everyone is preparing for the "unknown and unknowable" by facing a wide range of movements and time domains. Typically, athletes don't know the workout until it's posted online the night before or written on the whiteboard when they arrive at the gym.

"The Ranch," as it's known, was the venue for the 2020 Cross-Fit Games. It has been the home of other CrossFit Games, including the very first. All prior games include a run on the sprawling property. All of the preceding running events reduced athletes to crawling on all fours to climb some of the rugged and sandy hills. So, fans and athletes alike fully expected there to be another ranch run somewhere in the mix of tests for the athletes. When Castro announced a three-mile trail run around The Ranch, nobody was surprised. But nobody, especially the athletes, predicted what was coming next.

Just at the bottom of the hill, where the road turns right and flattens out, Fraser looks back at Medeiros and begins to sprint to the finish line. There was a small group of fans cheering and clapping. Dave Castro greeted an exhausted Fraser at the line and said, "Turn around and run it in reverse." Fraser, whose legs must have felt like Jell-O, was in utter disbelief. Unconvinced by Castro's pleading, he squats to catch his breath. Finally, Medeiros crosses the line, and Castro repeated, "Turn around and run it in reverse. I'm serious. I'm not joking." It was the twist nobody expected.

Both men, in utter disbelief, turned and headed back out to another grueling three-mile trail run in the hot California sun. "I thought it was a joke. He looked at me and said,

'You're going to start losing if you don't go!'" Fraser said of the twist thrown in by Castro at the last moment.

How do you react in these unknown and unknowable situations? What is your initial response when plans change, or you find out what you have been working on for weeks is no longer needed? Do you moan and groan? Do you need your boss to convince you to start over, or do you turn around and run back up the hill like the CrossFit champions?

How you frame the situation changes everything when it comes to adapting to change. Everyone has a Castro in their life, someone or something that throws obstacles in your way or adds twists you couldn't have predicted. You can't control the circumstances, but you can control how you prepare for those circumstances. One way is with an ancient mental model.

The stoic writer Ryan Holiday introduced me to the Latin phrase "Amor Fati" in his book *Stillness Is the Key*, which translates to "Love of Fate." He's built an entire industry based on the stoic principles of Cato, Aurelius, Epictetus, and Seneca. He sells a commemorative medallion to remind you how to make the best of every situation. "Treating each and every moment—no matter how challenging—as something to be embraced, not avoided. To not only be okay with it but love it and be better for it. So that like oxygen to a fire, obstacles and adversity become fuel for your potential." I read this to mean there will be the unexpected, and every moment is an opportunity.

We can learn a lesson from these professional fitness athletes. They spend all year physically and mentally preparing themselves for those precise moments of the unexpected. Of course, they don't know what will be on the test. Still, they know that they can expose themselves to various circumstances that stretch their tolerance for pain and suffering. (Are you ready for Surf Torture yet?) Their entire approach to fitness is designed to make them more adaptable to thrive no matter what is thrown at them.

~~~~~

Change is a part of life, and the rate of change is only accelerating. Being more believable requires you to be one of the fastest people in the room to accept new circumstances, unlearn what you believed to true, and prepare for the unexpected. It requires you to be more adaptable and drink the ants occasionally. You're going to need your newly discovered adaptability because next I'm going to ask you to let some fires burn.

CHAPTER 4

Let Some Fires Burn

———

It was our first vacation as a family, and it was worse than expected. My wife Jen and I have two kids. When they were ages three and five, we decided it was time for a trip. We had our hearts set on the volcanos, beaches, and the luaus of Hawaii, but Hawaii was too expensive, so we choose the next closest thing: Tampa, Florida!

If the fear of losing the kids on the beach or worrying they might drown in the gulf wasn't stressful enough, the fire alarm in the hotel went off three separate times. Try to picture your fellow bleary-eyed hotel guests stumbling out of bed and heading down the fire escape staircase in their nightgowns with half-packed suitcases in the middle of the night! It wasn't pretty.

When we arrived back at our home airport, we were exhausted, and my wife decided it would be most efficient if she went to get the car. That meant I would get the bags and the car seats and bring them to the curb. But before I could ask who was going to take the kids, she leaped down the escalator and vanished out of sight.

I had the kids in one of those giant double strollers. The five-year-old was freaking out. So, to avoid a scene, I let him play near the baggage carousel. (I know! Major dad fail!) The bags eventually came around the carousel. I was going back and forth between having a hand on the stroller, wrangling the five-year-old, and pulling bags off the carousel. I finally got the two car seats and four roller bags and had a hand on the five-year-old.

Next, I needed to get all the stuff and my kids seventy-five feet to the curb where my wife would meet us. I had more things than I could carry, so I started doing the inchworm strategy. I would move each item one by one and then run over and drag back the five-year-old. The operation went on for about five minutes before my frustration monster began to reveal itself.

Right when I was about to freak out and throw an adult tantrum in the airport, an elderly man walks up to me and says, "Bags or baby?"

"Excuse me?" I say.

He repeats himself, "Bags or baby?"

I reply incredulously, "No thanks, I got it."

With a reassuring voice, he says, "Son, you can't do this all on your own. You need help."

I nearly kissed his wise and wrinkled old face. Looking back on it, I probably should have said "bag" instead of allowing a stranger to leave the airport with my kid, but you take the help when you can get it.

Have you ever found yourself at work about to lose it because you're trying to do too much? As you progress in your career, you take on more and more with each promotion and new assignment. I've talked to all kinds of managers, and they all wish they had more time to do all the essential work and wear all the important hats in their life. Unfortunately, most are just like me at the airport, trying to hold it together just a bit longer in hopes things will slow down soon.

~~~~~

Kathy's new promotion was making her miserable. Kathy worked for a small healthcare company in Minnesota and moved from team member to manager. She managed a staff of administrators and nurses whom she cared about deeply. There was no management training, but she had been in the department for over a decade. So, she knew all the ins and outs of the department and all the personalities.

Joanne, her CEO, hired me to be Kathy's executive coach. She promoted her because she believed in her abilities. However, she was struggling to handle the responsibilities of doing the work and managing the people.

In my first conversation with Kathy, she seemed frazzled and overwhelmed. It was immediately apparent her compulsion to help the team was at odds with her ability to prioritize her work. She had quickly fallen into the routine of assisting the team all day and completing her work at home late into the evening. The new routine was hurting her relationship with her family and making her miserable.

Kathy was promoted because of her tenure, expertise, and work ethic. However, her newly visible stress and exhaustion were causing her to lose believability with Joanne, her team, and, most importantly, herself. She was beginning to question if she had what it took to be a leader.

From what you've read so far, you might be tempted to think this is a chapter on work-life balance. It is not. This is a chapter about increasing your believability with greater self-mastery. Being busy is a fool's errand. Confidence, composure, and clarity are rarely a result of burning the candle at both ends or fraying at the edges. I will give you some strategies for creating space in your day to be more effective. You will likely be skeptical of my recommendations (most are!), but I encourage you to try them first.

~~~~~

Perhaps this sounds a bit like your life. You leave the office feeling like you made a dent in the pile of emails that flooded in while you attended meetings all day. By the following day, the emails have returned and have multiplied. The precious thirty minutes that were open on your calendar yesterday? The time when you were going to go to the bathroom for the first time all day and eat the protein bar in your desk from 2016, return a few calls, catch up on your email, or even get ahead? That time is long gone.

Now you're double-booked for the meeting and the one after it. All you can think about is what you're going to miss at home if you work late, or worse yet, crack open that laptop after dinner. You might think to yourself, *there has to be a better way*, and as soon you get this one project done, you will figure it out, but it's heads down for now.

You are not alone. According to *Gallup's* Work and Workplace report in July of 2020, 40 percent of adults reported working more than forty-five hours per week, with 16 percent working over sixty hours per week. Don't forget the additional 52.7 minutes a day (mean average) for commuting. Together, this means 40 percent of adults in America spend somewhere between fifty and sixty-five hours working a week.

If you take the weekends and seven hours of sleeping per day, you only have thirty-five hours a week to bathe, buy groceries, go to the doctors, and spend time with family and friends. Do you really want to spend any more time working each week? Besides, do you think you're very believable when you're stressed out and overworked? Probably not so much!

~~~~~

John Pawlowski, a vice president of marketing and innovation at Bellisio Foods, is responsible for casting a vision and setting strategy for frozen product lines like owned brand Michelina's and licensed brand Atkins. He has a team of brand marketers and a supporting cast who rely on him to be strategic. In an interview, he said, "I realize I needed to help the team build a strategic thinking muscle and to create a strategic plan process... If I don't do this, it won't happen.

Everyone's just going to keep reacting and churning." He then said, "That's when I started carving out time."

John's approach was to block a couple of hours on his calendar two weeks out. When I asked him what he did in his first two-hour thinking block, he admitted, "I probably skipped my first three that were on my calendar." After several failed attempts, John decided he needed to hold himself accountable with a better plan. He promised himself he would go into a particular room, only bringing headphones, several notebooks, and a pen. To avoid temptation, he didn't bring his computer or his phone. When I asked him about the results, he says directly, "It's still a challenge because it's hard (work). But it's meaningful work, and I feel accomplished and satisfied when I'm done with it."

You might be wondering what he actually did in that quiet room with a notebook for two hours. We're going to cover that later in the book. What's important right now is creating the space.

John has famous companies following this strategy of taking time out of the workday to think. For example, Microsoft and Gates Foundation founder Bill Gates biannually takes an entire think week. A think week is where he locks himself away in a cabin with no contact with the outside world so he can read, think, and write. While he's there, all alone and free from distractions, Gates reads papers and reports while scribbling notes to himself for up to eighteen hours a day.

Successful companies take time off, too! Since 2015, outdoor retailer REI Co-op has closed its doors on its 168 locations in honor of its #optoutside campaign. REI Co-op wants to encourage its nineteen million members to spend their day outside with family and friends on Thanksgiving and Black Friday instead of shopping in their stores for new outdoor gear. In 2019, REI Co-op reported $3.1 billion in sales and more than 8 percent growth compared to 3.8 percent growth of the retail industry in the same year. So, REI Co-op closes its doors and it's the website on the most crucial shopping day in America. Its financial performance is nearly three points higher than the industry average.

The three examples above are meant to convince you to bet on yourself. By doing so, you give yourself a chance to be more believable and positively influence others. Then, with greater self-discipline and a longer view, you can take time out to think about your performance, thought process, and leadership of others. This investment is like sleep; you can only cheat yourself for so long before it begins affecting your performance. You may think you can survive on five hours a night, but trust me, everyone else can see it's taking a toll on your performance and quality of work. You get it, now the question is how?

~~~~~

I bet I can guess what you're thinking: "Jeff, that's nice for John and Bill Gates, but there is no way for me to make more space in my workday and get everything done that needs to get done." You're probably right.

You will likely have to let some fires burn. Reid Hoffman, a cofounder and executive chairman of LinkedIn, believes

"Smart entrepreneurs don't try to fight every fire. They have to let some fires burn—and sometimes very large fires."

In episode eleven of Hoffman's podcast *Masters of Scale*, he explains, "There will always be metaphorical fires." He categorizes some fires as sudden flare-ups that demand attention, and others slow-building fires happening in the background that will "spread if they aren't extinguished."

You've likely heard the phrase "firefighting" used at work to describe solving problems. The challenge for those who want to be more believable is you may miss critical opportunities if you spend all your time fighting fires. Hoffman describes the consequences as, "You'll be all reaction and no action." Believable people are thinking and planning to prevent fires. When they can't prevent them, they can discern between fires to let burn and those needing to be extinguished before they spread.

In the early days of PayPal, the customer service department was three people, and they were managing over ten thousand emails a month. Customers were frustrated and started calling the office directly, which eventually led to the phone ringing twenty-four hours a day, seven days a week. So, what did they do?

Hoffman says, "We turned off all the ringers on our desk phones and started using our cell phones for business." But, despite their mission of being customer-focused, they decided trying to respond to existing customers was taking away from satisfying future customers. He continued, "The problem is we have to treat the future customers, not just the current ones. If all we did was focus on the current ones, we'd never get to the future customers."

What was the result? "We let those complaints continue until one day, we were positioned to solve the problem all at once. We flew out to Omaha and set up a call center. Within two months, a two-hundred-person customer service department was up and running. Problem solved—and I wouldn't have solved it a moment sooner," said Hoffman.

The lesson here is there will always be fires to fight. Hoffman and his team would have never figured out a permanent solution for the constantly ringing phones if they had they not set aside time to think deeply about the problem. So, to think we can put them all out before making the important investments in strategy, leadership, and self-care is a farce. It's never going to happen. A better approach is to learn how to let some fires burn while you plant some seeds for the future by paying yourself first.

~~~~~

It's not too hard to convince people they need more time to think by letting some fires burn. But unfortunately, most people struggle to figure out how to do it when they have so many other demands on their attention. So, to answer this question, we need to turn to the first wealth-building lesson I learned before it was too late.

In 1926, George S. Clason published a book titled *The Richest Man in Babylon*. On page fourteen of the book is one of the greatest known secrets to building wealth: pay yourself first.

Clason's prescription for creating wealth is straightforward, "A part of all you earn is yours to keep. It should be no less than a tenth, no matter how little you earn. Pay yourself first."

Here's how most people spend their paycheck (well, at least how I spent mine before learning the pay yourself first principle): They receive their paycheck, pay their bills, buy groceries, spend a little on entertainment, and try to save a little of what is left. If you were like me, there was never anything left because there was always some unexpected expense needing to be paid. We tell ourselves better luck next month.

According to Clason's approach, you should do things differently. When you receive your paycheck, you should deduct at least 10 percent for savings (no matter how little you earn), then pay your bills, buy groceries, and spend what's left on entertainment. The outcome of this tiny amount of savings per paycheck Clason describes by saying, "Wealth, like a tree, grows from a tiny seed."

The only thing more valuable than money is time. Unfortunately, it's a limited resource, and more than likely, you've already spent a lot of it. However, you can use the pay yourself first method to manage your time and attention to spend it on the most important and impactful work.

Here is what happens if you pay yourself first and let some fires burn: you will have time to formulate a point of view. Believable people have a thought-out point of view on the organization. They can offer a balanced perspective on what's working and what isn't when trying to achieve its aims. To make a change or impact, you must elevate your thinking

with enough distance and perspective to see the interconnected and reinforcing parts of the system, processes, and
players.

Anyone can have a point of view, but only a few invest the
time to ensure their opinion and ideas are valuable and can
shape the organization. Your odds of success increase with
the amount of time you can pull yourself out of the firefighting mode. So, here are three ideas to help you pay yourself
first and do just that.

THREE MOVES YOU CAN MAKE TO PAY YOURSELF FIRST

The strategies I'm about to suggest will require a degree of
courage to pull off. I expect some initial skepticism from
anyone who feels their work calendar or email situation is
beyond their control. The recommendations are a bit bold, so
start small by running a few experiments first. Then, when it
works (and it will work), get a bit more daring. In the words
of Smokey Bear, "Only you can prevent work fires."

PAY YOURSELF FIRST

THIS MONTH

1	2	3 60 min strat. mgt.	4
5	6	7	8

DO YOU WANT TO ATTEND MY MEETING?

☐ YES
☑ NO

I AM
THINKING

THE PAWLOWSKI METHOD

Book 60 minutes
on your calendar
to think
strategically

SAY NO THANK YOU

Decline any
meeting that
isn't essential

CLOSE YOUR DOOR

Hang a sign
to let people
know

THE PAWLOWSKI METHOD

This is the approach John and countless others have taken to create some space for themselves. Open your calendar and skip two weeks into the future. If your calendar is like most people's, you will see some blank spots start to show up two weeks from now. Part of the reason is back-to-back thirty-minute meetings haven't landed on your calendar just yet. So, start filling in those blank spots with sixty- and ninety- minute blocks. Don't worry yet how you will fill those times at the moment; reserve the space now. I'm amazed at how people respond to this suggestion. They look at me with that "give me a break" skepticism.

Here's why it works: Let's assume your company uses Microsoft Outlook. Other people look at your calendar availability and see open slots, so they fill them with their agenda-less meetings. You receive an invite and don't want to offend anyone or miss anything that might be relevant to your work, so you accept.

Then you go to the poorly organized and pointless informational meetings and are frustrated because you could have used that time to get something valuable done. Even better, you bring your laptop to the meeting and partially listen while accepting future pointless meetings to keep the cycle going.

If you don't take control of your calendar, the masses will do it for you. Sure, some people will see your blocked time and invite you anyway. We will address that with the next recommendation in a moment. But most people will work to find an opening on your calendar and schedule a meeting during those slots. When they do, you've built some quiet time to think and work into your calendar.

If there are no gaps on your calendar two weeks out, go three or four weeks out. If you still can't find any, you need to read my following recommendation because you are saying "Yes" too often.

REPLY "NO"

Reply "No" to meeting invites. If I don't lose people with the first recommendation, I usually lose them with this one. At a certain point in my career, I found myself with way too much on my plate. I wanted everyone to believe I had everything under control on the outside. Still, I was stressed out, overworked, and overwhelmed by the volume of meetings, projects, and forecasts I was required to provide to leadership.

I was so overwhelmed and frustrated I just started replying "No" to standard weekly and bi-weekly informational meetings. I then expanded to any meeting where I wasn't a direct contributor or helping one of the project teams move forward.

If I wasn't sure about a meeting, I would default to a decline. If the meeting host asked why I declined, I would ask for the objective and agenda. They would typically say something like, "We just want to inform you about something," to which I would ask them to send me an email.

This approach may sound impersonal, but in fact, it's the opposite. I was no longer running from meeting to meeting all day. Instead, I spent quality time with people building deeper connections, which made me more thoughtful, strategic, and believable.

I'm not suggesting you ignore meeting requests with your boss; I didn't, but I did help convince him to cancel our weekly staff meeting in favor of a daily fifteen-minute stand-up meeting. By doing so, we avoided watching him go around the table so each of us could give him a status update. After a few months, my boss admitted he preferred the stand-up meeting over the staff meeting because he trusted us to do our jobs and ask for help when we needed it. He was only holding the meeting because he thought it was helpful.

Start small by declining one meeting next week to see how it feels. You'll likely find that nothing came of it, which will build your confidence in being more discerning with which meetings you accept and which ones you don't. Remember, no one cares about squandering your time and attention. If you don't manage it, no one will. However, they will judge you for being hurried, last-minute, overbooked, and frazzled, which are never ways to build believability. What you see as circumstances, they see as character.

To say "No" is to protect your future self from stress, anxiety, and frustration. In addition, doing so means you're giving future-you a chance to be more believable. But sometimes, even that isn't enough, which means we need to talk frankly about the misguided "open-door policy."

CLOSE YOUR DOOR

Kathy, from the story that opened this chapter, bristled at the idea of closing her door to get some work done. Like most managers, she wanted to help her people when they needed something. She didn't feel comfortable appearing superior to her team in any way. She also loved the connection and wanted to keep it. The thought of closing the door was just too much for her at first.

Closing the door, putting on your headphones, or getting to a quiet space are all ways for you to focus on the work you need to get done. Kathy was doing her work in the evenings, which took a toll, so we developed an experiment which helped her overcome the hurdle. She made a sign for her door that explained she closed her door to complete her paperwork. Kathy also added office hours during certain times when she was available for interruptions.

We framed closing the door with a sign as an experiment because experiments are designed for learning. It permitted Kathy to try on new behaviors in front of her team without feeling committed to them. If they served her and the team, she would keep them. If not, she could let them go without embarrassment. The results were immediate and profound.

What Kathy learned in the experiment was most people respected the sign. It turned out most were popping into her office with a question not because it was necessary, but because it just popped into their heads. In addition, several people on Kathy's team appreciated the clarity and complimented her on her new discipline.

These three moves are bold, and if you're like most people, they may make you uncomfortable, but all three are designed to help you regain control of your work experience. If they seem too much for you all at once, try to experiment with a few of the ideas. For example, put one block on your calendar or decline a meeting this week to see what happens. You'll be surprised how valuable even a little bit of space can do for your mindset, well-being, and believability.

~~~~~

My wife Jen, a former fitness trainer, has a sign in her gym for her clients that reads, "You can have excuses or results, but not both!" The truth is there is no respite on the horizon and no one coming to rescue you. The emails and the fires will continue to pop up; that's the nature of work. You will always have a reason to put off the investments in yourself, your team, and the company. The trick is to allow some fires to burn and pay yourself first by creating space to formulate your unique and valuable point of view.

If you followed my recommendations, you have a bit more room to breathe in your schedule. So, you can now focus your attention on transforming your thinking, which is the focus of the next part of this book. It begins by creating value with an owner mindset.

CHAPTER 5

Act like an Owner

"Act like an owner" was something I heard a thousand times before I learned what it meant. In May of 2017, I turned in my employee badge and walked out the front door for the last time. I thought I knew what it meant to act like an owner for seventeen years, but I was about to find out the hard way. I was going to become a small business owner.

According to the Small Business Administration, there are 30.7 million small businesses in the United States. In addition, small businesses employ 47.3 percent of United States employees. Based on data collected by the Bureau of Labor Statistics, if you open a business today, there is a 50 percent chance you will be out of business in five years.

Starting a business is exhilarating and terrifying at the same time. I was lucky to find a fantastic business partner and work that takes advantage of my skills and strengths. As of the writing of this book, our boutique consulting, facilitation, and coaching firm is in its fourth year and going strong. I'm optimistic we'll be around for years to come, but the facts are the facts.

If you started a business in 1995 (the year I graduated from high school—Go Rams!), there is only a 16.5 percent chance you're still in business today. The data says most businesses fail. I'm sure some fail for competitive and economic reasons. Yet, I'm willing to bet most fail because they broke one or more of the three must-dos of running a successful business.

1. Owners must act.
2. Owners must create value for customers.
3. Owners must get a return on investment.

Owners who want to increase their odds of success and their hopes of surviving follow the three must-dos of running a business. The same three lessons can significantly increase your believability at work. Following the three must-dos is a way to transform how you think and differentiate yourself from others. It works because the three must-dos better align your thinking and actions with leadership, owners, donors, and shareholders alike. Because, in the end, they all want you to act like an owner.

ACT LIKE AN OWNER

| 1. Give yourself permission | 2. Create value for customers | 3. Get return on investments |

OWNERS MUST ACT

"If you understand why you're here, and everything you do is with an owner mindset, then we can't lose," said Chris Dill, vice president and CIO at Kiewit Corporation, one of the top five construction and engineering firms in North America. Dill hired me in 2017 to help his leadership team craft new cultural pillars for the Kiewit Technology Group (KTG).

He described the mantra his team developed, which was to "create value with an owner mindset," as a one-two punch. The job to be done of KTG is to provide technology services and products to their internal customers, the people in the field who build dams, power, and petroleum plants around the world. But he said to "do that to any degree of success, what we really need is everybody pulling the rope."

The KTG leaders wanted to fight the inertia toward complexity and inaction. They wanted to remind employees of the goal, who they serve, and, most importantly, to act without waiting for permission.

I asked Dill to describe what the opposite of acting with an owner mindset might look like from his vantage point. It was the moment when an employee saw something and choose to do nothing. He said, "One of those things that are symptomatic in lots of larger organizations is where people are either not sure, or they're scared to step out on that limb a little bit and just make a decision."

He and the leaders wanted every employee to know they had permission to evaluate the circumstances and use their best judgment. He hoped to convey to the team of over four hundred employees that, "I'd rather you do something. Think it through, and even if it turns out poorly, I can live with it." This is a challenging hurdle for most employees to overcome because it seems to go against the hierarchy and chain of command in most organizations. But the most believable people are the ones who can act like an owner and navigate the company structure gracefully.

When you become a business owner, the first significant lesson (well, for me) was nobody cares, misses you, or knows they need your help. On my first day, I received no emails, no calls, and no leads. Three weeks later, nothing had changed. What was most disconcerting was we had built an excellent new website with a great logo. We even made cool stickers for your laptop and slick ball caps with our logo on them. Still, nobody called.

What dawned on me was the first rule of business. Owners must act, and by act, I mean initiate everything. It was up to me to reach out to anyone and everyone who would talk to me. I had to pitch our services and explain to people how I could help them solve their problems. Then, even when someone was interested, I would have to follow up repeatedly to close the deal.

Websites, logos, and marketing materials do not get clients or customers. Taking a risk by getting in front of people and asking for their business is what generates revenue. Unfortunately, anyone who runs a business and is struggling likely isn't talking to enough people. As an owner, I had to permit myself to look foolish, make mistakes, and fail miserably, otherwise, our new business wouldn't have survived until the end of the year.

The idea of permitting yourself to act may be a bit daunting if you're an individual contributor or a first-time manager. Still, it's essential if you want to develop your ability to lead at higher levels. Here's why you have to start right now: People who avoid action for fear of making mistakes or who don't trust their judgment never learn to overcome those mistakes or learn to trust themselves. It's a feedback loop, and you have to do it to get better at it. There's no way around it. If you want permission to lead and make big decisions someday, then you must start with whatever decisions are in front of you right now.

I wish I could give you specific advice on how to get started or what action you should take first. The truth is the best way to tell where you should begin is wherever you feel a little uncomfortable. The feeling of discomfort is your permission frontier, and the only way to push it further out is to spend more time right on the edge of it.

PERMISSION FRONTIER

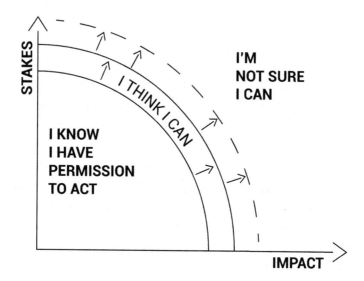

Start by leaning into the *ask for forgiveness* approach to see what you can learn. Will you make mistakes? Of course, you will. Everyone whom you're seeking permission from today makes mistakes, too. But with experience, they've just learned enough to recover quickly. You can, too, especially if remember the second must-do: owners must create value.

OWNERS MUST CREATE VALUE FOR CUSTOMERS

A red 1985 Ford pick-up truck sits inside a small storefront on the town square in Bentonville, Arkansas. The truck belonged to Sam Walton and is preserved just how he left it when he passed away in 1992. At the time of his death, the Walton family fortune was estimated at $23 billion in Walmart stock alone.

Walton was legendary for being customer obsessed. Stories abound of Walton being arrested in Brazil for measuring the width of store aisles; he thought they might know something he didn't know about cart traffic. He also believed the customer was always right. He once demanded a store manager not only exchange a defective lawnmower without a receipt but deliver a brand new one to the customer's home and mow his lawn!

Walton is quoted by Michael Kennedy in a Medium article as saying, "There is only one boss, the customer. He can fire everybody in the company from the chairman on down, simply by spending his money somewhere else." Walton's obsession for creating value for customers transformed retail and made Walmart one of the biggest retailers in the world.

When developing a strategy-building workshop to serve customers, I realized I was making many assumptions about what was most valuable to them. After my first workshop with a team of brilliant leaders, I quickly learned I needed to adjust my approach almost immediately. I had built the process and the activities all alone in my office. I had a bunch of theories and no experience on what customers needed from me.

I thought my role was to take them through exercises, but what I learned was I needed to help them think strategically, too (we will talk about this more in the next chapter). So, one of the moves I made was to build a six-part video tutorial with the five strategic questions explained in detail for the participants. As a result, when the next group of leaders arrived in a new workshop, they were more prepared and confident in being strategic. I had given them what they needed, even though they didn't know to ask for it, and as a result, the experience and the quality of the strategy they developed were dramatically better.

Value is the creation of something of worth or usefulness for others. It can include anything from assembling sprinkler heads on a manufacturing line, cleaning and stitching up a wound, or creating an advertisement that influences people to buy new tires for their minivan. It doesn't matter if you work for a for-profit or a socially-driven company. In the end, the goal is to create value for others.

Creating value for customers is the reason for-profits and non-profits exist. Yet sometimes this can be lost when faced with the challenges and friction of everyday work. Getting caught up in the details, tasks, and to-dos and losing sight of what is best for the customer is common. You've experienced this when you're about to order food or make a purchase at the counter and the person checking you out answers the phone. You probably think to yourself, "Seriously! I'm standing here with my credit card ready to purchase."

There is an endless list of ways to create value for others. What is essential for increasing your believability is creating value on two-time horizons, current-state value, and future-state value. Thinking on these two distinct time horizons will help you distinguish and prioritize the value you create.

CURRENT STATE VALUE

Take a look at your to-do list. There is a pretty good chance it has decisions and actions that keep the company (or nonprofit) running. It includes completing some work, responding to some emails, and finishing up the presentation you've been working on for weeks. All of the tasks create some degree of value, and if you didn't do them, the company would need to find someone else to do it. Some of it is urgent. Some of it is important. No matter what, it needs to get done.

Current state value is all the work that needs to be done to keep the business running today. It's helpful to frame how we think about this work on a continuum with accepting at one end and challenging at the other end. The distinction for how you approach current state value affects how others see you in the organization.

CURRENT STATE

ACCEPT	CHALLENGE
Focus on completing tasks	Focus on completing a task in more efficient and effective ways
How can I get it all done?	How can I get it all done faster or with better quality?

Accepting of the Current State

When you accept the current state, your attention is on identifying and completing all the tasks required. You may not spend too much time thinking about why the task needs to be done, just that it needs doing. You probably don't need to look too far to find examples of people in your organization who operate most of their time creating value in this area of the continuum.

Challenging the Current State

At the other end of the continuum is challenging the current state. It includes asking why we do things a certain way and not being satisfied with *because we've always done it this way* as the answer. It's challenging the status quo and pushing back on activities and behaviors that may or may not serve customers today.

Making a deliberate effort to spend more time and energy challenging the current state of serving customers will pay dividends. It's next-level work that will make you more believable, but it's only the first step on the journey. You must also work on creating value in the future, too.

FUTURE STATE VALUE

Now look at your 401K contributions. What percentage of your paycheck are you contributing? In an interview for US News, Shannon Nutter-Wiersbitzky with Vanguard said, "Typically, we would recommend a person save 12 to 15 percent of their salary for retirement." If you're like the average American, you are likely saving around 7 percent of your income for retirement.

What gives? We are talking about you in the future. I bet if I asked if you wish past-you had saved more money for today-you to enjoy, you would say absolutely. So then, isn't it logical to assume future-you would appreciate it, too? Thinking about the future is challenging because you must forgo thinking about what is urgent and important today.

F. Scott Fitzgerald once said, "The test of a first-rate intelligence is the ability to hold two opposed ideas in mind at the same time and still retain the ability to function." Working on the current-state and future-state continuums will increase the amount of value you can create for customers.

The future-state continuum represents how to approach the company's future and how you and your colleagues will create value for future customers in new and different ways. Like the current-state continuum, we can think about two extremes for thinking about the future state. You can approach the future state with pragmatic or transformational thinking.

FUTURE STATE

Pragmatic   **Transformational**

Seek incremental
improvements
in creating value

How can
we serve our
customers better?

Seeks new &
better ways
to serve new &
existing
costumers

What could
we do to serve
customers?

Pragmatic View of the Future State

First, you can think pragmatically about the future, which means you're sensible, realistic, and assume the future looks a lot like the most recent past. This might include assuming what customers need from our company will be the same or incrementally different two or three years from now. Think about baseball games. It feels pragmatic to me to assume people will still want hot dogs and cold beers five, ten, or fifteen years from now.

Spending any time thinking about the future state of your role, the team, the company, and its customers will give you a leg up on being more believable at work. The reason is by thinking about the future and value; you're aligning yourself with the vision of doing things better than they are today. This is valuable, but you can be even more useful with your thinking.

Transformational View of the Future State

You can also think transformatively about the future. Transformational thinking about the future state includes serving your customers differently and better than you do today. This is the highest level of value thinking because it is thinking creatively about what may not exist today. Transformational thinking is about providing value to customers in ways they may not even know they need today. You're probably enjoying some transformation thinking and don't realize it right now. It's an invention that changed the world.

The Sackett and Wilhelm's printing plant in Brooklyn, New York, had a problem. Summers in New York are hot and humid, making it challenging for anyone in the printing business in 1902. Willis Carrier was hired to fix it with his "Apparatus for Treating Air." With it, the air conditioning we enjoy today was born. According to Kirk Johnson, the Smithsonian's National Museum of Natural History director, the "air conditioner is America's greatest innovation." It changed America's geographic and political landscape because it allowed more people to move to southern and western states.

Carrier wasn't satisfied with fixing the humidity problem for Sackett and Wilhelm's. Instead, he envisioned a transformation for how people worked and lived more comfortably than they ever had before. He quickly took "manufacturing weather" from industry to the home. In 1914, the Charles Gates mansion in Minneapolis, Minnesota, was the first home to receive air conditioning. The rest, as they say, is history.

The ability to simultaneously think in the current and future state of creating value for customers gives you a complete picture of what creating value means. It's what Hoffman was doing by letting some fires burn in the previous chapter. The dual perspectives give you more insight into what is truly valuable to your customers and allow you to act in accordance. Now, there's one last must-do to ensure everything you do is worth it.

OWNERS MUST GET A RETURN ON INVESTMENT

Why do you go to work? Of course, money is a start, but it's probably not the only thing. You probably derive some form of satisfaction, challenge, social status, or a sense of belonging, to name a few of the non-monetary reasons. The ability to work and build a career can be a deeply personal and fulfilling experience, or it can be a miserable grind. It's all in the eye of the beholder.

Now let's think about it from the company's perspective.

What does the company see as your reason for coming to work? It's much easier to answer. The company wants to deliver the most value to customers, do it better than the competition, and do it in a way that generates a return on the company's investment.

The company wants to earn a high return on its investment. Therefore, it pays you in exchange for your talents, skills, and effort to maximize customer value, and it hopes you will deliver more value than what it pays you.

When we started the business, we had a simple rule for the first few years: no building, no inventory, no debt, and no employees. Why, you might ask? Because everything on that list comes with significant cost and it would make it challenging to generate a return on the time and money we were investing in the business. When you're the company owner, every expense matters. Intelligent business owners count every penny because every penny counts.

Big corporations think the same way but on a larger scale. I once had a manager tell me he expected a four time return on the investment in me. So, if he was paying me $50,000 a year, he expected me to generate $200,000 a year in value for the company. At the moment, I thought he was a jerk for being so direct, but now that I'm older and wiser, I agree with his logic. Even socially mindful or non-profit companies must get a return on investment, otherwise the entity will no longer exist.

Think about it like this: Let's assume the company pays you and Bob both $50,000 each per year in salary. Bob generates $100,000 of value for the company, and you only generate $35,000 value. How long do you think management or the owners of the company will continue the arrangement with you? Not very long!

This example is overly simplistic, and it's challenging to measure the precise value one employee can create for customers, especially if the employee doesn't work directly with the customer. However, this is a reality of how owners of companies think, and employees often forget it. Instead, owners think about the numerator and the denominator to drive a higher return on investment.

$$\text{RETURN ON INVESTMENT} = \frac{\textbf{BENEFITS} \text{ Profit or Social Impact}}{\textbf{INVESTMENT} \text{ of Time, Talent and Money}}$$

You might be turned off by all the finance and money talk about value and return on investment. An extreme focus on money may seem cold and overly calculated to you. However, return on investment can be expanded to non-profits and employees, too. The questions are different, but the logic is the same. How can we extract the most value from our investments? Here are two examples that don't have as much to do with money.

Bill Nunez, vice-chancellor of business and finance at the University of Nebraska-Lincoln, described how he leads a team of eight hundred using "lots of delegation, lots of trust, and lots of support." He explained leading a team of this size meant his role is to "support, nudge, and connect the dots," and he does it by asking, "What is best for the University?" and "How do our actions support and contribute to the mission?" His questions help him increase the return on investment for all the stakeholders involved—students, faculty, staff, state government, alumni, and the citizens of Nebraska.

Similarly, Steve Booker, president and CEO of SK Food Group, relies on the company's purpose to help him and the team ensure they are creating long-term value with everything they do. "Building a business focused on revenue growth, innovation, and increasing profit margins is unattainable unless we have the people in place to get us to the next level." He explained the vast majority of their associates are people of color and many are immigrants, which is why their purpose is to provide their associates an opportunity to support their families and personally grow.

The company manufactures sandwiches and wraps, premium charcuterie trays, and single-serve meals for many of the largest retail and foodservice operators in North America.

Their associates work in facilities that are refrigerated to preserve the ingredients and have over a dozen different languages spoken on their production floors. When faced with tough decisions, the SK Food Group leadership team asks themselves, "What is best for the long-term well-being of our associates?" This question guides the leaders, who aren't always on the manufacturing lines, to never lose sight of their purpose, which is the key to creating long-term value.

Creating value for these leaders at the highest level has little to do with what they produce on any given day. None of them are close enough to the customer to impact directly, so they rely on an indirect approach to create value. They count on simple principles and questions to help guide their thinking and behaviors to maximize the return on investment.

~~~~~

Knowing the three small business must-dos of acting, creating value, and getting a return on investment is the essence of acting like an owner. I learned these lessons from my experience in launching and running a small business. They are potent lenses for increasing your believability at work, and ones I wish I better understood when I worked inside a company.

Using these lenses to think about the current state and the future state of value will align your thinking with your organization's stakeholders. It's not always about money, but it is always about maximizing your investments. In the next chapter, we will explore the difference between working in the system and on the system. Doing so will help you take your believability to a more strategic level.

CHAPTER 6

Never Skip Leg Day

"It must be freestanding with the marshmallow on top." This is the last instruction I give to workshop participants about to embark on the Marshmallow Challenge. It's been a favorite of teachers and facilitators since the inventor of the challenge, Peter Skillman, shared it with the world at TED in 2006.

The object of the activity is to work as a team to use twenty pieces of uncooked spaghetti, one yard of tape, one yard of string, and one s'mores-sized marshmallow to build the tallest tower in eighteen minutes. Often a buzz of excitement fill the room when I ask the group, "Any questions before we begin?" It's fun to see grown adults so eager to compete for bragging rights among their peers.

As the clock winds down and the pressure mounts, several teams make hurried adjustments to their towers. Each team hopes their tower doesn't crash to the floor as I countdown the last seconds. Ten, nine, eight...one.

The most ambitious towers crash or begin to lean so severely they don't last more than a few moments. In a room of ten teams, I typically see one or two genuine contenders. After the laughter and jabbing quiet down, I begin debriefing the team to discover what they learned. Most teams conclude they miscalculated how challenging it would be to add the marshmallow in the game's waning moments.

Because it's a marshmallow, most teams mistakenly assume it's light enough to be added after they've built the tower. They spend the entire activity planning, debating, and building a tower. Some even forget about the marshmallow altogether. They are so engrossed in building the tallest tower they forget all about the objective: build the tallest tower with a marshmallow on top.

The Marshmallow Challenge is a beautiful exercise with lots of lessons to be learned about teamwork, communication, and prototyping, to name a few. Losing teams typically spend most of their time working on the tower and forgetting the marshmallow until it's too late. Winning teams recognize they must do both and keep reminding themselves of the objective.

~~~~~

"How do you think it's going?" asks the CEO of a software start-up company. We're standing outside overlooking the eighteenth hole of a golf course while on break during a two-day strategy-building meeting.

"You've got a sharp team here, and they're all in on the future of your company," I say as I watch a couple of golfers finish up their game with a few celebratory high-fives.

With frustration in his voice, "Yeah, of course. I know all of that already, Jeff. What I want to know is how do they compare to all of the other leaders you see in these strategy workshops?"

This isn't the first time I've had this conversation. It comes up nearly every time I facilitate a strategic planning workshop for a leadership team. It doesn't matter if it's a big company or a small one, the request is always the same: "Tell me how my team stacks up. Do you think they are strategic enough?"

I ask him, "You ever see those guys in the gym who have big and muscular chests, shoulders, and arms, but also have skinny chicken legs?"

He says, "Yes, of course. But what does that have to do with my team?"

"Like most of the teams I see in strategy offsites, your team is a lot like those guys at the gym. They spend most of their time building their upper bodies with long hours of bench press and curls because those are the muscles they can see in the mirror. Similarly, your team puts all their energy into getting things done as efficiently as possible because that's what is most rewarded at work."

I explain to him the guys in the gym with large upper bodies but underdeveloped glutes, legs, and calves don't do leg days. Most functional leaders have strong execution muscles but weak strategy muscles. The reason is they don't work their strategy muscles often enough to be as skillful as they could be. Therefore, they quickly fatigue when we ask them to use their strategy muscles. Like in the Marshmallow Challenge, most leaders focus on executing the work and lose sight of the marshmallow.

~~~~~

David Rooke and William Torbert published an article in the *Harvard Business Review* in April of 2005 titled *The Seven Transformations of a Leader* which provides research support for the CEO's intuition. They concluded what differentiates leaders is their "internal action logic," which is how they interpret their surroundings and react when their power or safety is challenged. Their research identified seven developmental action logics: Opportunist, Diplomats, Experts, Achievers, Individualists, Strategists, and Alchemists.

Of the thousands of people surveyed over twenty-five years, Rook and Tolbert found 55 percent of leaders fall into the Opportunists, Diplomats, and Experts categories and "were associated with below-average corporate performance." It shouldn't surprise you the Opportunists are looking out for themselves, and the Diplomats are more concerned with office politics than getting results.

It might surprise you to read the Experts, the largest group in the survey at 38 percent of leaders, achieve below-average results, too. According to the research, "Experts are great individual contributors...but as managers, they can be problematic because they are so completely sure they are right." This means over half of the leaders surveyed lack believability and thus lack influence in their organizations. In other words, they have unsightly chicken legs.

Another 30 percent of leaders are considered Achievers, who are significantly more effective at implementing organizational strategies. These are the managers "who both challenge and support...and creates a positive team and interdepartmental atmosphere." Achievers create a positive work environment, but the authors warn they may be challenged to "think outside the box." This group of leaders is more believable because they implemented strategy, created culture, and got results.

Finally, the top 15 percent of leaders (Individualists, Strategists, and Alchemists) "showed the consistent capacity to innovate and to successfully transform their organizations." The rare leaders who fall into this group challenge constructs, constraints, and perceptions. Individualists are master communicators and can adapt the message for their audience. The Strategists create a shared vision and can affect transformation at the individual and organizational levels. The Alchemists distinguish themselves from Strategists by transforming themselves and the organization in "historically significant ways." All the leaders in this group are the designers and drivers of change. Winning teams and organizations are built by these types of leaders.

If you aspire to be more believable, you aspire to be in the top 15 percent of the leaders surveyed. The differentiated skills that make you more believable are communicating, being strategic, and transforming yourself and the organization.

Being more strategic leads to greater believability because it is rare and valuable in any organization. It means you understand the organization's current state and can envision a better future state and have the skills to articulate the transformation required to get from here to there.

For our purpose, being strategic means you can generate individual and organizational transformation. You can see it. You can help others see it, and you can lead people to reaching it. In other words, you're the kind of leader who never loses sight of the marshmallow because you never skip leg days.

THINKING ABOUT SYSTEMS

The microphone clicks on and a voice repeating the words, "Ladies and gentlemen, the captain has turned on the fasten seatbelts sign," comes from the speaker above your head. You've heard this a thousand times, and it barely registers as you return your attention to the book you were reading or the movie you were watching.

Something else that may barely register with you is the aircraft you're flying on is a system of systems. A flight control system allows the pilots to steer the aircraft. The landing system keeps you from landing in a ball of fiery wreckage when you return to Earth. Avionics help the pilot know where they are going. Finally, the environmental controls pacify passengers who take for granted the purified air at a near-perfect seventy-two degrees for the entire flight from New York to Los Angeles in under six hours.

You also might not recognize the airplane is also part of a complex system. It includes air traffic control, support trucks, baggage-handling equipment, satellites, and radars to keep the nearly one hundred thousand flights taking off and landing daily around the globe. "All of the travel—from the time you leave your home until you arrive at your destination—can be considered a system of systems." According to Purdue University's College of Engineering, "This emerging system-of-systems concept describes the large-scale integration of many independent, self-contained systems in order to satisfy a global need." Thus, everything from the global supply chain, your body, and the company you work for is a system of systems. This means we need to think at the system level if we are going to think strategically and increase our believability at work.

Using the current-state and future-state value continuums from chapter five, we can set up two helpful categories for thinking about what you do at work. At any point in your day, you can work in the system or work on the system. Knowing the difference will create more value for customers and increase the return on investment. By raising your awareness of both types of work, you are thinking about the spaghetti tower and the marshmallow.

WORKING IN THE SYSTEM

When you work in the system, you are working within the assumed constraints of the system. You're following the rules developed by someone else long ago. It's doing what you were hired to do. Most individual contributors work in the system, but many managers do, too.

In chapter five, I shared with you how value creation happens on two distinct time horizons. Working in the system is the combination of accepting the current state and being pragmatic about the future state of the business. (See the diagram below.) The goal is to complete the tasks and projects required to keep the business running. This is the type of work most people do to run the business. It's working on what is directly in front of you and what is most immediately visible. It's day-to-day problem-solving that goes on in most organizations.

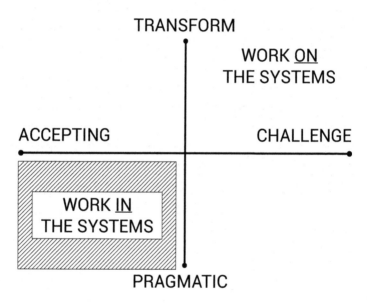

Working in the system is valuable because if you don't do it, nothing will get done. Customers aren't served if you don't do the work of producing products or delivering services. Therefore, most people in your organization should spend most of their time working in the system.

Questions you might ask when working in the system are:
- What is the situation?
- What is the problem we are trying to solve?
- How can we get it done most efficiently?
- What matters most right now?
- What is within my responsibility?

The questions above are valuable, but only asking these types of questions will not differentiate you from others in the organization. The reason is they don't challenge or help the company transform into something better and more valuable for customers. Asking these questions leads to a perception of dependability, which is excellent. Still, it won't result in you being more believable with leaders and owners. There's a great parable of doing things without questioning its value that illustrates the point:

> *A favorite family recipe for a holiday ham had been passed down through the generations. As the mother was making the ham for the umpteenth time, she was teaching her newly married daughter how to make their family's ham.*
>
> *She carefully cut both ends off the ham, set it in the pan, and added the secret combination of spices. Her daughter, who was taking notes, asked, "Why do you cut off the ends?" Her mother answered, "Because that is how my mother taught me to do it."*
>
> *Later, the mother began to wonder why they cut off the ends, so she asked her mother. The grandmother answered, "You don't need to cut off the*

ends! I always did that because my old oven was too small for a big pan."

The challenge with only working in the system is losing sight of the marshmallow and waking up someday and realizing you have chicken legs. You spend most of your career preserving the status quo and never questioning why the company does what it does or how to do it better. To increase your believability, you must work on the system, too.

WORKING ON THE SYSTEM

Working on the system requires approaching work with a different perspective than working in the system. Working on the system requires thinking about value in the current state and future state in the opposite way you do when working in the system. When working on the system, you are both challenging the current state of the business and thinking in a transformative manner about the future state. It's keeping the marshmallow in mind and challenging yourself to keep it on top of the tower the entire game.

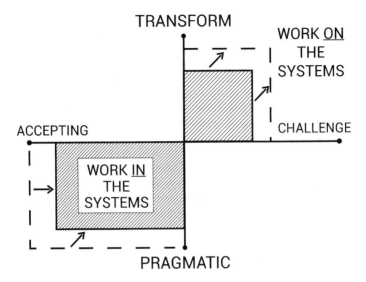

To do it well, you must do what, in *A Survival Guide for Leaders*, Ronald Heifetz and Marty Linsky coined as "getting off the dance floor and going to the balcony." It's a visual metaphor that captures the action of stepping out of the system and asking, "What's really going on here?" It's my go-to phrase in strategy-building workshops to remind leaders we are strategic and not tactical.

One of my favorite examples of going to the balcony where leaders can look down on the system of systems of their business is a story told by Brian Chesky, founder and CEO of Airbnb, about creating an eleven-star experience. Chesky describes it in a Masters of Scale podcast. He and his team challenged themselves to apply the standard hotel rating system to the Airbnb home-sharing experience.

First, they asked themselves what would be a five-star experience for an Airbnb guest? You knock on the door and someone lets you in—pretty basic.

Then the Airbnb team raised the stakes by asking themselves, what might be a nine-, ten-, and eleven-star experience? Chesky described the eleven-star experience as showing up at the airport, and the host is there with Elon Musk and tells you, "You're going to space."

The point of the exercise is to imagine new possibilities for impressing customers. Working on the system is strategic and creative, and it helps you use a broader lens of what may be possible. Even if, in the beginning, it isn't pragmatic.

Chesky credited this activity with creation of the Airbnb's experience offerings in 2016, where guest can select anything from surf lessons, foodie tours, photo shoots, to forest bathing when you arrive at your host destination.

Working on the system pushes you to define value for the customer in new and different ways. For example, it might include thinking about new customers or new ways to serve existing customers. In addition, it can involve thinking about how the organization is structured and resourced with talent and capital.

To work on the system is to assume nothing is permanent or out of bounds strategically. The customer, value proposition, capabilities, and systems are all levers you can pull in your quest to generate the most value. Operating from this vantage point has the advantage of not needing to worry about the many details of the system. Instead, you can better see the interconnected and interrelated parts of the system all at once.

From the balcony, you can challenge the current state and think transformatively about the future. When you work on the system, you rely on a different set of questions:

- What is in scope and out of scope?
- What would be most valuable to the customer (internal or external)?
- What will matter most in the future?
- How can we do this better tomorrow?
- What can we learn from this experience?
- What can we eliminate or stop to make us better?

Without understanding the concept at the time, I recall a moment when I briefly worked on the system rather than in it. It was my very first professional role, and it was in the insurance and loss control department. I was the finance analyst, which meant I was responsible for the production of reports. Each month, I had a list of reports I was supposed to run and email to people throughout the company. It was tedious and unrewarding.

On one occasion, and out of frustration, I ran my reports like I had done every month before. However, this month, I decided not to send the reports and not say anything about it to my boss. As you can probably guess, nobody noticed. I repeated the experiment three more times before I stopped producing the reports altogether.

Months later, I told my boss about it, and he just shrugged his shoulders and said, "Well, you better be ready to work quickly if they ever ask about the reports." But, of course, they never did, and I saved six hours of drudgery each month.

The challenge of working on the system is it requires you to step out of day-to-day working in the system, which, like a screaming baby, can be hard to ignore. You might even be skeptical it's even possible to spend all day working on the system. But the good news is you don't have to go from giving 0 to 100 percent of your time to this task. Instead, you can begin with a little bit of time each week by stepping out of the fray, putting on your headphones, or closing your door. Not sure what to do with those stolen minutes? Don't worry. I got you covered.

HOW TO WORK ON THE SYSTEM

Remember the Pawlowski method from chapter four, where you block an hour to work quietly without distractions? You should spend this time thinking about how you can do things better and different for your customers, or think about improving the internal systems and processes of the company.

Need a few ideas to get started? Here are three guaranteed topics that will generate value regardless of what industry you're in or if you work for a for-profit or a non-profit.

Ideas that generate more revenue or reduce costs

You may not love finance, but thinking about creating more income or decreasing costs will always be valuable. The ability to challenge and improve the effectiveness of the company's sales process or make the company more efficient will make you more believable with the leaders and owners of your organization.

Examples:
- Ideate ways to network with more potential customers.
- Look at your calendar for the last two weeks and make a list of everything that didn't add value. What can you do to eliminate it in the future so you can work on more valuable tasks?
- Think about the activities you do repeatedly. How can you develop a checklist or a process to make it effortless?

Ideas that will make your customers' lives better or easier
Companies exist to provide value to customers. If you can find new and better ways to delight your customers better than the competition, you are instantly creating more value than the next person.

Examples:
- Make a list of everything you've heard your external or internal customers say, good and bad. What can you do to expand or address the feedback?
- Interview your customers about what you should keep doing, stop doing, and start doing to make their lives easier or better.
- Identify all the little extra moments that might surprise and delight your customer and show them you understand them better than your competition.

Ideas about the future and how you might cross the chasm between the current state and the future state

Setting a vision for the company, your department, or your team is a compelling approach to being more believable. Asking yourself how we could operate as a group to deliver value can multiply your impact on others.

Examples:

- Capture in writing your role, team, department, or company five years from now and describe in vivid detail how it might look if it were two-times, five-times, or ten-times better than it is today.
- Explore what the "real value" is you create in your role by describing the functional and emotional benefits you provide your customers.
- Describe what would have to change between how things are today and what it would take to transform into the person, team, department, or company that could deliver on your vision of the future.

So, you might be wondering to yourself, "Are you telling me I should stop working in the system and work exclusively on the system?" Absolutely not. Only a few people have the luxury to spend their days working on the system as a full-time job, and let's be honest, they are likely out of touch with reality. I suggest to be more believable, you must spend more time working on the system than you do today. One additional hour per week thinking about where you and your team fit into the system and how you can make it better in the future will pay huge dividends.

~~~~~

Most people think about the tower and forget the marshmallow. Many fail to recognize the difference between working in the system versus working on the system, resulting in a bad case of chicken legs.

Working on the system is like leg day in the gym. It isn't sexy, and it requires a lot of hard work, the result of which you may not see in the mirror right away because it's a long-term investment. It likely means you must let some fires burn today to prevent more significant fires in the future.

Sadly, most leaders confuse time in meetings or titles with being strategic, and they couldn't be further from the truth. You may be born with the gift of natural intellect, but how you think is also a skill.

Like adding some leg days into your workout routine, the more strategic thinking you do, the stronger you will be at generating individual and organizational transformations. Being strategic is a big topic. In the next chapter, we will define strategy and making choices more deeply so you feel confident in making the right choices.

CHAPTER 7

Become the Mountain Climber

—

The God Committee earned its nickname because they decided who lived and who died. A seven-member panel included six men and one woman. Their occupations were varied and included medicine, clergy, labor, legal, and home-making. The original committee was formed in 1961 to identify from thousands of Americans suffering from kidney disease the nine recipients of life-saving dialysis treatments at Seattle's Swedish Hospital.

The University of Washington's Dr. Belding Scribner developed a new Teflon shunt to make dialysis a safe and regular treatment. It could expand the life-saving treatment from weeks to years. The challenge was more people needed the treatment than the Settle Artificial Kidney Center had machines. The panel was formed because Scribner felt selecting the candidate for treatment was a social choice rather than a medical one.

The committee members were unpaid, and their identities were kept anonymous. Together they considered all types of factors like marital status, net worth, occupation, education, church attendance, and the number of dependents when reviewing eligible candidates. According to resident scholar of the American Enterprise Institute Sally Satel, the ultimate question for the committee was who should be saved, "the person who contributes the most to society or the one whose death would impose the greatest burden on society, in the form of children left without care or resources?"

The story above is about choices, difficult choices. Should the doctor who invented the life-saving technology get to decide who lives or dies, or should regular citizens? Should the committee select candidates at random or carefully consider the person's social worth? Answers to questions of this magnitude do not come easily.

Fortunately, many of the choices we make in our daily lives rarely include such grave consequences. Still, making choices of any kind can feel daunting. Whether it's as mundane as what we should we have for dinner or as important as deciding if you want to have children, choices of every size and scope include the benefits of the choice but also the trade-offs. Of course, nobody wants to make the wrong choice!

~~~~~

On a more personal level, the Four Burners Theory vividly describes the choices we make as adults. I first learned about this metaphor from the blog of famed author James Clear, who traced its origins to a David Sedaris article in The New

Yorker. The metaphor of the four burners helps to frame what it takes to be successful and is fun to play at parties with friends. Here's how Clear explained it:

Imagine a stove represents your life with four burners on it. Each burner symbolizes one central quadrant of your life.

- The first burner represents your family.
- The second burner is your friends.
- The third burner is your health.
- The fourth burner is your work.

The Four Burners Theory says "in order to be successful, you have to cut off one of your burners. In order to be really successful, you have to cut off two."

I like to think of the Four Burners Theory as the grown-up version of the game *Would you Rather?* I fondly remember playing the game with college buddies on long road trips and asking questions like, would you rather fight one horse-sized duck or one-hundred duck-sized horses? The point of the game is to force you to choose between two impossibly tricky options. The resulting answers were often laughably awkward. The Four Burners Theory forces you to think deeply about your goals and actions and, at the same time, declare what you are willing to sacrifice.

~~~~~

Choice creates the tension that makes life and work interesting. Most choices aren't always life and death, as with the God Committee, but the most meaningful choices can be incredibly challenging, if not downright gut-wrenching. In the previous chapter, I encouraged you to invest more time working on the system. It's a choice you have to make if you want to be more believable at work. By doing so, you are choosing to be strategic instead of tactical. You choose to operate from the balcony instead of on the dance floor, which is easier said than done.

"You're not strategic" is something I heard from people who didn't believe a finance guy like myself could make it as a brand manager. They assumed because I had only ever supported the business, it meant I couldn't run the business. Several people predicted I would be back in finance within the year. They believed being strategic was a natural-born talent rather than a skill you can develop. (Challenge accepted!)

If you've made it this far into this book, then I'm guessing you are someone with a growth mindset. As beautifully explained by famous blogger Maria Popova when describing Carol Dweck's research, "You see failure not as evidence of unintelligence, but as a heartening springboard for growth and for stretching our existing abilities." The good news for you is you're right! Being strategic is a skill that can be developed with the right attitude and effort.

As hard as it was for me to hear, most of the naysayers about my strategic abilities were correct. I had no idea what it meant to be strategic when I got the job. However, I believed it was something that could be learned.

I had only made the expert and achiever transformations from the Rooke and Tolbert's study (chapter six) up to that point in my career. I would have to define better what strategy really is, why it matters, and differentiate it from other types of thinking and planning if I was going to make it as a brand leader, and later as a strategic planning facilitator.

When it comes to being strategic, the challenge for most managers and leaders is the same one I had to overcome and is threefold:

- They don't distinguish strategy from other forms of planning.
- They don't consider enough options. (Chapter 8)
- They aren't clear about their choice. (Chapter 9)

Using the Pawlowski method to find time in your week to think and set your intention to work on the system is an excellent first step to overcoming these challenges. You are making space to think and are focused on the right kind of questions. The next step is to be better at defining strategy and choices to differentiate this thinking from other types of thinking. Doing so will help you organize your thoughts to be more effective, clear, and strategic.

WHAT STRATEGY IS (AND WHAT IT IS NOT!)

When asked to lead a strategic planning offsite for a company, I always request to see the current strategic plan. Unfortunately, I typically get one of two types of documents representing a misunderstanding of what strategy is. The first type of document consists of the company's mission, vision, and values. The second type of document includes goals, objectives, tasks, metrics, and owners. Both documents are valuable, yet they miss the mark when it comes to strategy.

To help you better define strategy, I'll share what I share with the leaders at the beginning of my strategy-building workshops to provide a straightforward framework for strategic thinking. This framework demystifies strategy and more clearly distinguishes it from Aims and Operating Plans. Of course, it's not perfect, and it isn't robust enough to get you a job at McKinsey Consulting. Still, it is a big step toward being more believable.

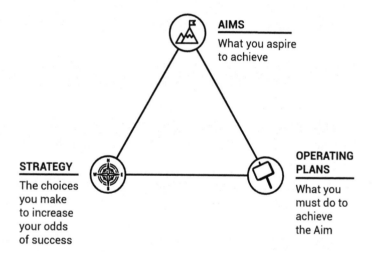

AIMS
What you aspire to achieve

OPERATING PLANS
What you must do to achieve the Aim

STRATEGY
The choices you make to increase your odds of success

Sometimes it's easier to learn something by learning what it's not. With that in mind, I'll start by defining Aims and Operating Plans. I will then describe Strategy so you can see why it's different from the other two types of thinking.

AIMS

Colorado has fifty-three 14,000-foot peaks. Each of them is majestic, and reaching the top is challenging for everyone. According to the Institute for Altitude Medicine, "At 14,000 feet, the air has 43 percent less oxygen than at sea level." As a result, your heart rate will elevate, and you will feel short of breath as you climb steep grades to the summit. Everything you do feels more laborious, but the views are outstanding.

In the simplest terms, Aims are what the company hopes to achieve. The Aim is to pick one of those 14,000-foot peaks and declare it's the mountain we will summit together. Aims can include terms like the north star, the big audacious goal, mission, vision, and values.

A clear Aim provides the company with a focus and purpose for employees and customers. It is a choice because by selecting one of the mountains to climb as a team, you simultaneously say we will not climb any other mountains. However, it's not the only choice.

Aims are an essential component of strategy but not "the Strategy" itself. The challenge for many leaders is they love to linger in this type of work. It allows them to continually fiddle with the perfect vision statement rather than making strategic choices. It's also common to see leaders who think their work is done because they've developed a vision statement. Huge mistake.

Dr. Paul Batalden's famously stated, "All organizations are perfectly designed to get the results they get!" I once had the president of a manufacturing company that generated $10 million in revenue a year tell me he wanted his company to be a $50 million company in five years. My short answer was you would have to make different choices because today's choices fall $40 million short. He wanted to focus all his energy on refining the Aim when he needed to focus on the strategy.

An organization's Aim describes the future state and underlying values for what it aspires to be someday. It's the equivalent to looking toward the Rocky Mountains and selecting one mountain to climb. It doesn't, however, choose anything that will help you climb the mountain. That's where a Strategy and Operating Plan comes in handy.

OPERATING PLAN

If the Aim defines the mountain to climb, the Operating Plan gets the entire team from the base to the summit. It includes the milestones, measures, people, tools, and resources needed to achieve the Aim.

The operating plan is the daily distance objectives, the map with mileage markers, and checklists to ensure we have all the right gear to move together efficiently from one milestone to the next as we summit the mountain. Without a clear operating plan, summiting a worthy 14ner is a dream and likely won't be realized, at least not by you.

Leaders who love details and believe in the maxim "What gets measured gets done" enjoy this type of planning because it's reassuring to plan every detail and step to achieve objectives. Operating plans are different from Strategy because they focus on the internal actions and to-dos rather than describe the company's transformation.

A risk when building the Operating Plan is to become too married to it. I once had a leader share with me a detailed monthly three-year plan written in great detail. Imagine yourself investing so much time and energy into building this plan and how upsetting it might be to learn COVID-19 would change everything about work for twenty-two months.

STRATEGY

At this point, you might wonder what else might be left to plan for our journey to the summit. The Aim provides the goal to focus the organization's energy. The Operating Plan provides what to do and when to do things. The Strategy, on the other hand, is about transforming yourself and your company into mountain climbers.

Of the fifty-three 14ers in Colorado, seven are classified as *most difficult*. With a distance of seventeen miles and an elevation gain of 5,300 ft., Capital Peak is widely considered the most difficult. To climb it, you must pass the infamous Knife Edge, which climber and blogger Matt Payne describes as "rugged, exposed, loose, and dangerous." In his ranking of the toughest 14ers, he says of Capital Peak, "There are very few breaks to be had, and simple mistakes can and do prove to be fatal." Capital Peak requires climbing experience and skill to summit. It also includes a long and arduous backpacking trip to reach its base.

Alternatively, families with strollers can reach the summit of another 14er, Pikes Peak, via the Cog Railway. At the top, they can enjoy freshly fried donuts as they take in the views. However, mountains like Capital Peak demand you become a different kind of climber. You must develop more strength, skill, and capabilities to summit mountains of this caliber successfully.

In chapter five, Rooks and Tolbert defined Strategists as leaders who generate individual and organizational transformation. The Strategy or Strategic Plan describes the transformation. It includes getting in top physical shape for the mountain and developing your climbing capabilities before you begin the hike up the mountain. For organizations, the Strategy is when leaders choose the transformation to become the company capable of achieving its aims and doing it before the competition does it first.

The Strategy is the set of choices that help transform the organization or individual so they can reach the Aim. Being strategic is the capability to identify and make the essential choices that enable an organization or individual to increase their odds of success. The case study below is an example of both.

CASE STUDY

Special Olympics Nebraska (SONE) is a non-profit near and dear to my heart. It provides athletes like my son, Brady, an opportunity for competition, camaraderie, and personal growth. In an interview with Carolyn Chamberlin, president and CEO of Special Olympics Nebraska, she shared the many strategic choices SONE needed to make to reach its Aim of transforming the lives of seventy-five hundred people with disabilities in the state of Nebraska.

Choice #1: Where should SONE focus its resources?
A. Traditional sports and activities exclusively for people with intellectual disabilities.
B. Unified sports and activities designed to bring people with and without intellectual disabilities together.

Choice#2: How should SONE finance itself?
A. Lots of individual donors whose contributions can add up quickly.
B. Few big corporate donors who make large donations and grants.

Choice #3: What services should SONE offer to its customers?
A. Just sports and activities for the athletes.
B. Sports, Health, and Education services.

Choice #4: How should SONE provide the services?
A. Build a large professional staff to put on sporting events and leagues.
B. Keep a small staff that relies on a group of motivated volunteers.

Choice #5: Where should SONE offer its services?
A. Statewide so everyone has an opportunity to participate.
B. Only large metro areas where most people live and work.

When combined, these five choices can shape and transform Special Olympics Nebraska into an organization capable of reaching their Aim of transforming the lives of seventy-five hundred people with intellectual disabilities. There are no right or wrong answers to these choices. It's up to the organization's leaders to make the choices that put the odds in their favor.

The choices don't define the summit or the steps for achieving it. Instead, they describe who the organization must become. By choosing one option for each of the choices, they are saying no to the other option, which is an essential element of strategy.

For example, when considering Choice #1, SONE chose to pursue Option B—Unified Sports—because it would reach more participants and positively impact stereotypes and change mindsets as people with and without intellectual disabilities play on the same team.

SONE's strategic choice involved partnering with other organizations that could help move the effort forward. The Nebraska School Activities Association (NSAA) oversees high school championships and could reach schools across Nebraska much more effectively than Special Olympics.

Building the partnership with NSAA required SONE to move off the dance floor and onto the balcony by setting standards and procedures with the NSAA and then letting their partner do what they do best. This strategic decision created a pathway to broaden the reach of unified sports and activities and impact the culture on school campuses.

It took five years before hosting the first Unified Championship event, but that one decision changed the course of Special Olympics Nebraska and has created opportunity. Chamberlin predicts one day unified sports in high schools will no longer be unique, and instead will be the norm. "When I think about that single decision, I am overwhelmed at the potential of the impact of that one decision," said Chamberlin.

Non-profits work on very tight budgets and do not have the luxury of research funds or beta testing. Therefore, finding strategies that will allow the work to get done prudently is paramount. Leaders must be willing to let go and relinquish control. To reach schools with this unified initiative, partnering with the NSAA was the best way for SONE to accomplish their Aim.

A strategy can and should be written down, but it is not a document. It isn't something you put in a binder and stow away on a shelf. Instead, a strategy is a set of choices that can be used to make better decisions about what you should and should not do. Like a compass, it's a tool to keep you on course and increase your odds of achieving your aims.

~~~~~

When you combine all three types of planning, you have a recipe for clarity and alignment, which is needed to execute even the most modest plans:

1. **Mountain:** An inspiring Aim focuses the team's energy on a common goal and identity.
2. **Mountain Climber:** A clear Strategy describes the transformation the company and the team must make to reach the Aim.
3. **The Plan:** A detailed Operating Plan describes the work that needs to be done to deliver the strategy.

Most leaders I've worked with have one or two of these types of thinking down. Having all three gives you a tremendous advantage in being more strategic and believable. The ability to distinguish between Aims, Strategy, and the Operating Plan is a differentiator all by itself. Strategic thinkers are rare and thus more valuable. Sharpening this skill will go a long way toward making you more believable at work.

A line spoken by helmeted and chain-mailed Grail Knight from the movie *Indiana Jones and the Last Crusade* has stuck with me since I was thirteen years old: "You must choose. But choose wisely." Indiana Jones searched for the Holy Grail, and if he found it, he could save his father. Make the right choice, and the hero prevails. The next chapter is about exploring enough options so you make the right choices.

CHAPTER 8

See like the Hummingbird

——

Hummingbirds are awe-inspiring and graceful creatures. With wings that beat eighty times per second, they can hover in one place. Their mere presence can delight just about anyone. They often surprise you by zooming in and out on their endless search for nectar. There are many reasons to admire hummingbirds, and you can add seeing things that are invisible to humans to that list.

Scientist and researcher Mary Caswell Stoddard and her team at Princeton University tested the wild birds. They discovered hummingbirds could see ultraviolet light. Human eyes have three color cones which can see light with wavelengths between four hundred and seven hundred nanometers. Within those three hundred nanometers is every color of the rainbow. Beyond that narrow range, it's invisible to the human eye. Hummingbirds have a fourth cone which allows them to see ultraviolet light.

Stoddard is quoted saying, "Humans are color-blind compared to birds and many other animals," in a news release of her team's work. What she means is birds perceive colors that exist in the natural environment that humans cannot see. In the paper her team produced for the National Academy of Science, she said, "Our analysis of plumage and plant colors shows that—for tetrachromatic animals—nonspectral colors are likely important for communication and foraging." By seeing a broader view of colors, birds have a competitive advantage when looking for food. They see more options.

You may remember the electromagnetic spectrum from a high school science class. It's the diagram of a line including the various wavelengths of energy with a small portion highlighted as visible light in the mid-section of the line. The visible light is all the light we can see with our human eyes and includes red, blue, green, violet, and purple.

ELECTROMAGNETIC SPECTRUM

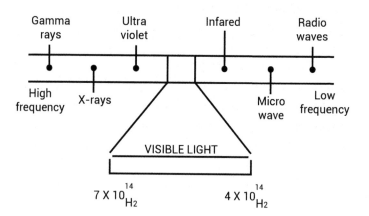

What makes the electromagnetic spectrum interesting is everything we can't see. We know these lights exist because of people like Sir William Herschel, who discovered infrared in 1800, Johann Wilhelm Ritter, who discovered ultraviolet light in 1801, and Maxwell and Hertz identified and proved the existence of radio waves in 1887. There is more non-visible than visible light on the electromagnetic spectrum. The same phenomenon is at play when we're making choices; we have many more options than we naturally explore.

~~~~~

See if this sounds familiar to you. You attend a meeting where the group is tasked with making a choice. Someone throws out an idea to which the rest of the group begins to quickly dissect it. One person says it will never work because we tried it before. Someone else proposes the opposite idea. Someone begins drilling into the many steps it takes to pull it off. Finally, someone else brings up an entirely different topic that has nothing to do with the problem at hand. After the allotted thirty minutes, someone looks at their watch and says, "Oh, I'm late. I have to run to my next meeting." Everyone else in the room jumps up and does the same. The problem is not solved.

Though my scenario is a little snarky, I'm sure you've experienced something similar. What I notice time and time again in strategy or innovation workshops or one-on-one executive coaching is most people aren't strategic because they don't consider enough options. It's something that has driven me crazy for years as a strategic facilitator and coach until one day I discovered something brilliant: a line.

A line is defined as a long, narrow mark or band, but it is so much more than that. Like the electromagnetic spectrum, it can represent all the possibilities seen and unseen for solving a strategic problem.

Like many eureka moments, I discovered the line out of frustration in a strategy workshop I was leading in Kansas City, Missouri. It was a cramped, windowless conference room with a group of sharp leaders. There had been lots of discussion in the morning session, but I struggled to help the team resolve anything. At lunch, I explained to Nicole, my cofacilitator, what bothered me the most was it seemed like we were having five different conversations at once.

After lunch and before the leaders returned to the room, I drew five lines on a flip chart to represent the five conversations from the morning. At the end of each line, I captured the extreme options for each of the topics. When the leaders entered the room, I explained the lines and asked them to place a sticker on where they stood for each of the issues discussed in the morning.

Some of the topics were in unanimous agreement at one end of the line, and it was easy to see we no longer needed to discuss. However, other lines needed more nuance, so the team introduced several additional options between the two extremes and placed them on the line. By the end of the workshop, the leaders were confident they explored all their options and were clear on all five of the choices made by the team.

Note to the Reader: When I say I discovered something, I am not saying I invented the concept of considering multiple options between a set of extreme possibilities. When I use the word discovered, I only mean to say I found the practical power of framing options on a line through a first-hand experience. Roger L Martin and Jennifer Riel wrote the book Creating Great Choices, which beautifully describes integrative thinking. This book, for me, was next-level meta-thinking and is beyond what I'm describing here, but it inspired my thinking. Any genius you may find below is from Martin and Riel. They expanded my mind to see the immediate value when helping a room full of leaders.

FIVE STEPS TO EXPLORING YOUR OPTIONS

A client of mine, Chris Alford, VP of International at Home Instead, has nicknamed the option line as strategy toggles. Anytime we start a project together, the first topic of discussion is to set up the toggles. We use the toggles at the beginning of projects to help us decide how we will frame up our strategic options and considerations later.

Alford calls them the toggles because he thinks of them like the toggles on a mixing board you might see in a music recording studio. As a sound engineer, you can turn up or turn down different sounds in search of the best experience. Adjusting a toggle in one direction has an impact on the other choices we make. You can't just turn all the knobs up to one hundred. It is this tradeoff that makes a strategy come to life. We do this intentionally because knowing what you're trying to decide and how that decision impacts other choices helps keep us strategic. It also helps bring others in the organization along on this journey by understanding the implications of a strategic decision before the organization moves forward.

I'm going to share five simple steps to using the toggles to consider more options, leading to more decisive choices. To help you visualize it, I will give you a business challenge to think about while I walk through the five steps.

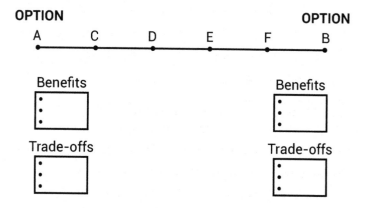

Problem: You decide you are going to go into business for yourself doing something you love. There is only one problem: you live in a rural town in southeastern Kansas with around nine thousand residents. Oh yeah, and it's 1956, so there is no internet, mobile phones, birth control, communication satellites, or barcodes to scan merchandise because none had been invented yet. Of course, you wouldn't know you needed any of these inventions at the time. The best things you have going for you are a little bit of money and a whole lot of passion.

STEP 1: FRAME THE PROBLEM

Not that you should ever stop here, but I believe all problems can eventually be summed up with a "So, it's between option A or option B" statement. When a person or a group reaches this moment, they have framed the problem in its simplest terms so everyone can understand it. A group doesn't understand the problem until they can say, "It's between option A or option B."

Once you reach this point, you can draw a line on a flip chart, whiteboard, or piece of paper. You should have a line with option A at one end and option B at the other. You must really draw the line. Don't imagine it or assume everyone sees it as you do. Trust me, if you keep it in your head, it loses 95 percent of its power. It's just a line. You can do it! I believe in you. Once you have made the line, you are ready for the next step, but first let me introduce you to Dwayne's Photo.

In 1956, Dwayne Steinle lived in Parson, Kansas, and decided to open Dwayne's Photo, a photo processing store. The problem for Dwayne was he lived in rural Kansas, a two-and-a-half hour drive from the area's largest metropolis, Kansas City. When he opened the business, a Kodak representative warned there weren't enough people in his area to succeed.

What is the strategic problem to solve? *To attract enough customers to your store so you can make a living.*

- **Option A** = Take the advice and don't open a photo processing store in rural Kansas.
- **Option B** = Open a store and hope the Kodak guy is wrong.

STEP 2: CONSIDER THE NUCLEAR OPTION

If you remember the hummingbird and electromagnetic spectrum, you know there is more on the line than humans can naturally see. If you don't see a nuclear option, which can be do nothing or blow it up, you are not considering all the options, and you may need a longer line. I once had a conversation with a coaching client that illustrates my point:

Client: "I'm not happy in my job, and I feel stuck. I need your help."
Coach: "Okay, let's consider some of your options."
Client: "I don't have many options."
Coach: "Grab your stuff and walk out the door right now!"
Client: "I don't like that option, but I could do this..."

When people say they don't have any options, what they really mean is they don't like their options. Once the client knew he had at least one option, he could almost immediately see several other options. The options he proposed were less extreme than walking out the door and more satisfying than accepting things the way they were. By the end, he told me he had a whole new sense of control over his situation because he now had options. Those options, like ultraviolet light, had been there all along.

Strategic people always include walk away, change the game, or break the rules options on their line. These are the most extreme options you consider, and they remind you that you always have options, even if many of them are ones you don't like. Now that you have the real extreme options on the line, you can consider more options.

Look at your line labeled with option A and option B. Now, ask yourself if one of these options is the nuclear option, meaning the option that could blow everything up? Let's go back to Dwayne's Photo for a moment:

Problem: To attract enough customers to your store so you can make a living.

- **Option A** = Take the advice and don't open a photo processing store in rural Kansas.
- **Option B** = Open a store and hope the Kodak guy is wrong.
- **Nuclear Option B** = Pick up and move his family to New York City, where millions of residents live and take photos.

Moving to New York City may not be extreme to you but imagine if you're a guy living in Parsons, Kansas, in 1956. It would probably be pretty outrageous to him and would be his nuclear option. Having this option just extended the line and made decision-making more strategic because it expands the number of options available. You're now beginning to see like the hummingbird. Let's reveal more by expanding your options.

STEP 3: EXPAND YOUR OPTIONS

Now that you have the true extremes on your line, you are now ready to play with various options in between the two extremes. Ask yourself or the group what might be some novel and new ways of solving the problem anywhere along the continuum? It is the reason I asked you to draw the line. You and the group can see the options on the line to identify new possibilities that are either left or right of the previous option.

At this point, you're splitting options or creating new ones on the spot. There is likely an infinite number of options possible. Try to develop five or six options, even throw in a few silly ones. (You might be able to turn a silly idea into a good one.) Once you have several options, you are now ready to move to the next step in the process. Let's explore some of the hypothetical options for Dwayne's Photo in 1956.

Problem: To attract enough customers to your store so you can make a living.

- **Option A** = Take the advice and don't open a photo processing store in rural Kansas.
- **Option B** = Open a store and hope the Kodak guy is wrong.
- **Nuclear Option B** = Pick up and move his family to New York City, where millions of residents live and take photos.
- **Option C** = Try to be the cheapest processor of film in the world.
- **Option D** = Borrow a bunch of money and buy out all the other film processors in America to corner the market.
- **Option E** = Specialize in rare and hard-to-replicate film processing.

Between the two extreme options, there are countless variations to consider. There is no right or wrong answer here, and where you place the options on the line is up to you. Considering multiple options in this way is powerful because it means you are identifying real options. Too many managers and leaders who come through my workshops with a habit of not considering enough options. This exercise forces leaders to visualize their creativity more. Doing so helps them be more strategic with their thinking.

STEP 4: NARROW THE FIELD

It's now time to switch from expansive to contractive thinking. Typically, it's pretty easy to identify the options that don't show much promise without a lot of work. If doing this exercise in a group, you can give each person an opportunity to add a dot or tick mark next to the option their gut tells them is the best option, like I did with the leaders in Kansas City.

Here is another moment where you must visually capture where you or everyone stands on the options. By capturing people's instinctual best choice, you make everyone show their cards. No one can say the group didn't consider their option or they disagreed but didn't say anything later. When you have the best two or three options identified, you're ready for the final step. By getting all this on the whiteboard, you are getting it out of your head, which is a powerful step, and we will talk about it more in the next chapter. Let's now sort the hypothetical options for Dwayne's Photo into two categories.

Poor Options:
- **Option B** = Open a store and hope the Kodak guy is wrong.
- **Nuclear Option B** = Pick and move his family to New York City, where millions of residents live and take photos.

- **Option C** = Try to be the cheapest processor of film in the world.
- **Option D** = Borrow a bunch of money and buy out all the other film processors in America to corner the market.

Attractive Options:
- **Option A** = Take the advice and don't open a photo processing store in rural Kansas.
- **Option E** = Specialize in rare and hard-to-replicate film processing.

Even at this point in the process, I like to move quickly and listen to my gut. Several options don't seem viable to me at first glance, but that's why this is the time to capture in writing where everyone stands and then have a thoughtful discussion about it. You want to feel good knowing you didn't go with the first option and didn't waste time overthinking all possibilities.

STEP 5: FLESH OUT THE CONTENDERS

Each option is a potential choice, and making choices will help you be more strategic and believable. The reason you make a choice is you want the benefits of that choice. At the same time, you want to recognize what you must give up by choosing the option.

For instance, let's say you and I meet for lunch. (Okay, I'll buy this time!) When you order a salad with dressing on the side instead of the juicy double cheeseburger, you are choosing the benefit of feeling better later in the day than if you would have devoured the burger. However, it came with a cost because you traded the immense joy and satisfaction of the cheeseburger for the raw broccoli and dry lettuce. Every choice comes with benefits and trade-offs. (Hint: If there are no trade-offs, you're not making a choice, which is a choice to achieve mediocre results.)

The final step in the process is to list the benefits and trade-offs of each of the final options. Three or four bullet points should suffice for each option. The trick is to advocate for each option, meaning you want to place yourself in the mind-set of believing in the option, then repeat for each alternative considered. Half-heartedly going through the motions isn't considering your options and misses the point of the exercise. Let's see what might have been the benefits and trade-offs to Dwayne's Photo as they contemplated launching a new business.

Option A = Take the advice and don't open a photo processing store in rural Kansas.

Benefits:
- Zero risks of losing your money.

Trade-offs:
- Don't fulfill your dream of owning your own business
- Miss the opportunity to work in film and photography all day
- Nothing to leave your family when you're gone

Option E = Specialize in rare and hard-to-replicate film processing.

Benefits:
- Fewer competitors
- Make your store a destination
- Build a reputation as the place to go for most discerning photographers

Trade-offs:
- Requires specialized equipment
- Must develop a highly specialized staff
- Technology can disrupt the marketplace

A person can use as much rigor as they please when defining the benefits and trade-offs of each option. I like to do a quick estimate first, knowing I can always go back later and dive deep into proving to myself one of these options is better than the other.

So, what happened to Dwayne's Photo? Dwayne Steinle chose to specialize in rare and hard-to-replicate film processing. Mr. Steinle passed in 2020, but his business in Parson, Kansas, has defied the odds and lives on today.

Dwayne's Photo was the center of attention of the photo world in 2010 for being the last processor of the famed Kodachrome. It was beloved by photographers and Paul Simon for its vivid colors. Kodak announced it would stop producing the chemicals required for processing Kodachrome film. Dwayne's Photo would be the last to process it. Dwayne himself processed the very last role. It included pictures he captured of loyal customers and employees at the end of an era. For weeks and months leading up to December 4, 2010, people from six continents sent hundreds of thousands of roles through the mail or pilgrimaged to hand-deliver their film to the little shop in Parsons, Kansas. Not bad for a shop thought to be located in an area too sparsely populated to be successful. Good thing Dwyane considered his many options instead of listening to the Kodak people.

~~~~~

This was a long chapter to say you should first draw a line and add some dots to it when faced with a problem. It sounds overly simple, but I've found it to be one of the best tools in my arsenal when helping leaders be more strategic. Considering your options in a disciplined way, even if that means drawing a simple line with dots on it, will make you more believable. Leaders in your organization will recognize the depth of your thinking and trust your judgment and recommendations. Like the remarkable hummingbird, you can see what is invisible to others when considering all your options. Now you are ready to make the call.

CHAPTER 9

F.O.C.U.S. On Decisions

"We're aligned. I think we can move on," said Pete after twenty minutes of vigorous debate between him and Megan, two senior leaders in a strategy building workshop at the Lied Lodge in Nebraska City. The discussion started innocently, but the tension escalated into a standoff. The ten other leaders had become spectators as the two slugged it out with their competing ideas.

Pete was confident he made a winning argument. Megan nodded in agreement with Pete's suggestion to move on while she uncrossed her arms and looked satisfied with her victory.

I questioned how aligned the two leaders could be since they seemed to argue for two approaches which were polar opposites.

"Fantastic. Would you both humor me by writing down the choice you both just made?" They looked at me incredulously and reluctantly wrote down what they believed was their shared agreement.

"Please hold them hold up so everyone can see."

Both Pete and Megan were stunned to see they had made zero progress. Neither of the leaders had moved their position. Both assumed their argument had won over the other person. It was a thirty-minute discussion with great points and counterpoints with no decision to show for it.

You are probably familiar with this scenario. If not the specifics, you've most definitely experienced the aftermath if you've concluded a meeting believing the team was aligned on a decision for what to do next. You later hear someone explaining the choice and next steps to someone else and wonder what meeting they attended. You think to yourself, "That's not what we decided." Or worse, you learn weeks later someone wasn't aligned, yet didn't say anything in the meeting. Instead, they chose to ignore the group decision and do whatever they wanted.

Two chapters back, we covered the different kinds of choices with our mountain metaphor. With it, we disentangled Strategy choices from Aims and Operating Plan choices. In the last chapter, we explored more options with a simple procedure of using the toggles to see the invisible options. Now, I will help you dial up your effectiveness and believability by providing tools to help you facilitate decisions for yourself and others.

The enemy of choice is two-fold. First, leaders aim for consensus instead of decisions. Second, leaders don't use tools or frameworks to guide them through making a decision. Both are easily overcome with a lightweight process and are the focus of this chapter because recognizing choices and making decisions is essential if you want to be more believable at work.

~~~~~

The words consensus and decision are thrown around often in the work environment. Sometimes they are used interchangeably on the assumption they mean the same thing. However, the definition of consensus is a general agreement, while a decision is a conclusion or resolution reached after consideration. Consensus may be how a team arrives at a decision, but they are not the same thing.

What is interesting is according to Google Book Ngram Viewer, usage of the word consensus has increased 242 percent since 1960, while the word decision has only increased 5 percent. Usage of the word consensus has even outpaced the growth of the word team, which has grown 150 percent since 1960. Reaching a consensus as a team is how work gets done today, but the collaborative approach can have drawbacks.

Krista McDonald, EVP and chief strategy officer at Farm Credit Services of America and Frontier Farm Credit, described in an interview how consensus is highly useful for effectively gathering feedback and insights from the individual members of the team, but relying on it exclusively is problematic because reaching a consensus leaves the "door open to come back." What she is getting at is teams reach a consensus or general agreement of what they should do next. Yet, because the group didn't officially decide, team members can return to the topic again and again.

The analogy she gave me for differentiating between reaching a consensus and making a decision illustrates it beautifully. Imagine how easy it might be to reach a consensus that we should visit China. But, deciding we should do it is different than calling a travel agent, purchasing tickets, and getting on an airplane to visit China. The former is consensus or general agreement we should visit China; the latter is a decision because it's followed by action. She said, "In business, you want to act on the things you decide on, not say we should do it someday," and added, "Consensus discussions must end in a decision."

Think back to the scenario that opened this chapter. The setting for this discussion was a strategic planning offsite where the leaders knew they had two days to explore options and make choices. Both parties had great ideas and offered compelling perspectives, yet all the talking didn't lead to a decision. After two days with them, I can assure you they are good at this stuff, but even they stopped short of a decision.

The first step for anyone wanting to be more believable and make better decisions is recognizing reaching a consensus is not a decision. The second step is to use a lightweight framework to deliver a decision. The remainder of this chapter is dedicated to helping you facilitate decisions by yourself or with a team.

~~~~~

One of the reasons meetings are notoriously ineffective is because many leaders lack process and, as a result, aren't clear on the choices they're making. Like Pete and Megan in this instance, most leaders keep topics, discussions, and decisions in their heads, where they also keep their feelings, stories, memories, and everything else in their lives. It's like they put the decision in the junk drawer in their kitchen, expecting to easily find it the next time they need it. Unfortunately, our memories aren't as reliable as we think.

Elizabeth Loftus of the University of California-Irvine studies what is known as false memory. In an article for *Slate Magazine*, Loftus said "We all have memories that are malleable and susceptible to being contaminated or supplemented in some way" in an interview with Alison George, as she describes how people's memories are fallible and that we are prone to making things up.

When asked how this happens, Loftus describes the process as combining experience from different times and places when we try to remember something. She says, "Bringing it all together to construct what might feel like a recollection but is actually a construction."

Memories are collections of experiences and emotions wound up together, and the act of recalling them can change the story. Imagine how those memories might get mixed up, lost, or entirely made up when a person goes from meeting to meeting all day. Assuming you can keep all the decisions throughout the day in your head and free of error is what you might call an avoidable failure.

"Avoidable failures are common and persistent, not to mention demoralizing and frustrating," writes Atul Gawande, a surgeon and Harvard professor who promotes the benefits of a checklist in his bestselling book *The Checklist Manifesto.* "We need a different strategy for overcoming failure. And there is such a strategy—though it will seem almost ridiculous in its simplicity, maybe even crazy to those of us who have spent years carefully developing ever more advanced skills and technologies. It is a checklist."

Using a checklist requires humility to recognize you need a tool to help you walk through a set of predetermined steps. Pilots and doctors must be highly skilled and experienced to earn their professional licenses, and even they don't trust themselves not to make mistakes or skip essential steps. Both use checklists for pre-operations and pre-flight because they understand the stakes. They could cost someone their life.

F.O.C.U.S. DECISION-MAKING FRAMEWORK

I built the following F.O.C.U.S. decision-making framework to help workshop participants quickly make better and clearer choices. Don't underestimate its effectiveness in helping you make choices because of its intentional simplicity. I built it with the belief that complicated tools are rarely used.

There are five questions to walkthrough as a team or alone. Don't just talk about it; write it down. If there is a debate, then create a draft for both choices. The goal here is to remove the subjectivity, document what we know and think today, and reveal gaps in understanding or misalignment.

FOCUS FRAMEWORK FOR DECISION MAKING

F ACTS — What are the facts of the situation?
1.
2.
3.

O PTIONS — What options are you considering?
1.
2.
3.

C HOICE — What option are you choosing?
1.
2.
3.

U NDERLYING ASSUMPTIONS — What assumptions are you making?
1.
2.
3.

S TEPS — What steps are required next?
1.
2.
3.

I recommend you push the pace as you go through this exercise. Set a timer to answer all the questions with a "done is better than perfect" mindset. Once you've answered all the questions, you can gather more information or make refinements.

FACTS OF THE SITUATION

What are the facts of the situation? It is a question I often use in one-on-one coaching and group settings because it has a powerful way of focusing the conversation. When you ask someone to describe what's going on, they will color it with all sorts of opinions, stories, feelings, and gossip. However, when you ask people what the facts of the situation are, they suddenly tighten up their description.

For instance, let's suppose you have an underperforming employee at their job and you want to give this person feedback. I mention this scenario because it is one of the most common challenges in executive coaching conversations. If you came to me with this challenge, I might ask you to tell me about the person and how they're underperforming. If you're like most people, you might describe the person's history of behaviors and attitudes. You would also likely include how they make you and others on the team feel. You might even speculate why they are behaving in a certain way. You might share your philosophy on how to behave at work and how you don't understand why they would do things differently. You would likely describe it much like you would a movie from beginning to end.

Alternatively, what if I ask you about the facts of the situation? You would likely filter out everything but the most essential from the description and list off a few bullet points.

- He is a talented and dependable person who has a lot of potential.
- However, he is always late to meetings and disrespectful of me and others.
- His behavior is beginning to hurt team cohesion and morale.

The first description is colorful and entertaining. The new description is more objective and to the point. The former might be up to debate; the latter is harder to argue and thus more helpful when trying to decide what to do next.

When completing this first step, set the bar pretty high for yourself or the group. Challenge yourself to write the facts down as if you were a disinterested third party with a thirty-thousand-foot perspective. Take the view of an impartial judge and jury rather than from the defendant facing jail time. What would the judge say are the facts? Framing the situation in this way will allow you to let go of past baggage or how we got here. List the facts in bullet points. Aim for three to five straightforward fact statements to set the stage for the choice you wish to make. Now that you have the facts in hand, it's time to consider your options.

OPTIONS CONSIDERED

With a clear sense of reality, it's time to consider your options. I'm sure you think you're pretty good at assessing your options, but once again, if you're doing it in your head, then you're not considering options. Getting the options out of your head and on paper so everyone involved can see them will help you treat the options objectively.

Use the options toggles introduced in chapter eight. Start by identifying the extreme ends of the continuum. Then, if no possibilities come to mind, ask yourself two questions: What is the nuclear option? What if we did nothing? Rarely will you not have options. Instead, you intuitively ruled those options out because you didn't like the trade-offs or consequences.

It's wise to heed the Heath brothers' advice from their phenomenal book Decisive and avoid settling for what they call "either-or choices." Instead, they suggest you should aim for three to five distinct possibilities before making a choice. To make the point, the Heaths' shared a story about Alfred Sloan, the long-time CEO and chairman of General Motors when he once interrupted a committee meeting with the question:

"Gentlemen, I take it we are all in complete agreement on the decision here?"

Everyone nodded.

"Then...I propose we postpone further discussion of this matter until our next meeting to give ourselves time to develop disagreement and perhaps gain some understanding of what this decision is about."

Suppose you or your team find it easy to reach a consensus without exploring any additional options. In that case, you may be missing an opportunity to make a better choice. Don't settle for the first good choice you hear. In workshops, I often remind participants, "Consensus is not required." I'm trying to remind them consensus is not the aim when we are exploring options. Disagreement and skepticism can be healthy and helpful in making better choices.

Once you have three to five options on your line, add benefits and trade-offs for each. Regardless of which one your gut tells you is the correct choice, force yourself and your team to flesh out each choice as if it's the best choice. It requires a bit of humility and curiosity, but you might discover something previously invisible to you.

If someone tells you they don't have enough time to weigh all the options or go through this process, remind them you're trying to make the best choice, not one to revisit again and again. It can be tempting to accept the very first option presented. But do the work, and you will raise your strategy IQ tenfold.

CHOICE

With genuine consideration of all the options, you are now ready to make a choice. I like to start with a simple straw-man poll using a thumbs up or thumbs down for each of the options. The vote will identify the front runners from the weaker options. From here, you can ensure everyone understands the choice, discuss each option's merits, and take another vote or test the waters by making a recommendation.

If a clear choice isn't evident, now might be a good time to use the three P exercises developed by my friend and long-time colleague Chris Routh, sales director at Conagra Brands, to "frame risk by putting words around it." Then, add a value to each option by asking if each option's desired outcome is possible, plausible, or probable. The way Routh explained it, "Anything is possible, but you'll need a whole lot of luck on your side." Plausible outcomes include "facts and combinations of elements that will hold up to logical scrutiny but haven't been broadly proven through experience." Probable outcomes are the ones most likely to happen and will pass most "tests for reasonableness."

For instance, let's say you own a small coffee shop that serves fancy single-origin and locally roasted coffees. Your landlord has increased your rent, and you are considering a price increase on the coffees you sell to your customers. Your three Ps exercise might look like this:

- **Possible** = To your customers, your coffee is as essential as oxygen and Netflix (Netflix is right up there with air, right?). Therefore, they will pay any price to drink the black gold you serve every morning.

- **Plausible** = Okay, so some of your customers are casual fans, but almost all of them are superfans. You might lose a customer or two, but nothing to worry about because you have great customer service, so you will hardly even notice them.
- **Probable** = Yes, you have a hardcore group of loyal customers, but you also have casual and price-sensitive customers. Odds are the casual customers might visit the store less frequently. Many, if not all, of the most price-sensitive customers will be lost to the Dunkin' Donuts down the street.

Now you have risk-assessed your best choices, narrowing the options down to one or a couple of finalists. You might find yourself in a situation where you don't like any of your options. I call this an "Argo moment," inspired by the Ben Affleck movie Argo, where Affleck poses as a movie producer to rescue six Americans in Tehran when the CIA director is presented with a recommendation:

> CIA Director: *"You don't have a better bad idea than this?"*

> Jack O'Donnell: *"This is the best bad idea we have, sir, by far."*

Sometimes you don't have any good options, but that doesn't mean you don't have options. You might need to more deeply explore your best lousy option.

If you or the team is still struggling to make a choice, it's likely a gut feeling you can't explain. You may not like the choice but have difficulty explaining why. Roger Martin, former dean of Rotterdam University, widely considered one of the top strategic minds, uses this magical question to get unstuck when trying to make a choice: "What would have to be true for this to be the right choice?" I love this question because it flips obstacles on their head and makes them actionable. I've witnessed dozens of leaders list out the impediments to a choice and realize that many are not genuine obstacles or are easily overcome.

Another option if you find yourself in one of these moments is to "loosen your grip" on the choice you're trying to make. I once struggled with painful hand cramps during Brazilian jiu-jitsu sparing sessions that left me nearly unable to drive home afterward. I asked my black-belt professor Dennis Bacon what to do about it. In all his Zen-like wisdom, he said, "Loosen your grip." He taught me to stop fighting my opponent for a certain hold on their gi collar and to release and find a new grip instead.

When it comes to making a choice, we tend to act as if everything is on the line and it's the last choice we're ever going to make. In other words, we hold on too tightly. People have been making choices for thousands of years, and they will likely continue to do so for thousands more. Make a choice and move one. You can always make another choice later.

To complete this step for yourself or as a team, you must write down your decision. I like to write the word decision and under it a single sentence that describes our choice. If in a group, I then read it aloud and ask the group, "Is this the decision we are making right now?" If it isn't, we make tweaks and rewrite it until we agree. You should also take the flight attendant approach when speaking to the people in the airplane exit row by looking at each individual and asking for verbal confirmation. It's silly, but it does save you from someone coming back later and saying they didn't agree to the decision.

UNDERLYING ASSUMPTIONS

Because you and the team have decided, it might feel like an excellent place to stop, but you will miss out on the learning step of the process if you do. I call it the learning step because most of us have short memories when making choices. You're ahead of most because you have been writing things down, but you also want to take a moment to provide some insights for you (or the team) to understand your choice better and why you made it.

Annie Duke, cognitive psychologist and world champion poker player who's won $4 million at the tables, warns of a phenomenon called resulting in her book *Thinking In Bets*. Resulting is when a poker player makes a bad bet and gets a great result and then believes it was a good decision because of the outcome alone. For instance, let's say someone dives headfirst into a river without checking the water depth beforehand and doesn't get injured. This is a bad choice by all measures. However, your buddy might assume because nothing terrible happened, it was a good choice.

Duke on *The Steve Pomeranz Show* explains, "Our biases lead us to think that if we have a successful outcome, we've made a good decision, but if we have an unsuccessful outcome, it's bad luck. People also tend not to take the blame for their own mistakes and, therefore, do not really move forward in learning how to be more successful."

So, before you move on to action, write down the assumptions you and the team made when making the choice so you can return later and learn about your decision-making and improve it for the future. In the postmortem of the decision, you can ask yourself: Did you get the results you intended? Was it because of the choice you made? What new information did you learn? What information was previously available but was missed?

There is no way to know everything you need to know to make a choice, so you will always make some assumptions. Capturing the assumptions in writing for posterity allows you to recognize your biases so you can be better next time.

STEPS REQUIRED
Strategy without execution are just words on paper. It doesn't change anything until you act on the choice. When I managed the Banquet Frozen Meals business, our team took a year and a half to earn approval to transform the entire business. We would make significant food improvements, add new products, change the packaging, raise the price, and begin advertising for the first time in a decade. It was a massive undertaking to get approval from the executive team.

When we received approval, we accomplished something few had ever done before. The entire team walked with our heads held high back from the CEO's office to our little cube farm, and then it dawned on everyone that we hadn't accomplished anything. It would take another year and a half to get the changes into the market and another year to understand if we had made the right choices.

Take a moment now that you have decided and identify the three to five significant milestones of implementing your choice. Remember what Krista McDonald said earlier in this chapter, "In business, you want to act on the things you decide on, not say we should do it someday." If you don't have a plan of action, then all you really did was reach a consensus, and, "Consensus must end in a decision." The significant steps or milestones you identify don't need to be a detailed weekly Gantt chart. Instead, it should paint a picture of what it's going to take to see your choice and resulting change come to life.

~~~~~

Pete, Megan, and the rest of the leadership team went through the steps I described for you above and were able to align on a set of choices that have served the company well for years. Working in teams and consensus decision-making feels like it's here to stay. You can elevate your results and your believability by using this lightweight process and helping your team make better decisions. All that is left to do now is to get out of the way!

CHAPTER 10

Get Out of the Way

——

Her years of excellent performance earned her a promotion to the role of president, and it was the same reason she was struggling to do the job well. Leah Vetter, area president for Arthur J. Gallagher, had been in her new role for a little over a year before hiring me to be her executive coach. Our aim was for me to help maximize her performance in the role. Prior to the promotion, Vetter was an outstanding sales performer known for her ability to close deals. It was easy to see during our first official meeting Vetter was a high performer who had a strong desire to win and honestly cared about the team.

Vetter asked me to conduct a series of 360-stakeholder interviews with her boss, peers, and key employees. In all, I conducted five interviews and developed a themes report to review with her. Reviewing the themes report with clients is always a bit tense. They are excited to discover more about themselves, yet nervous about learning something they would rather not know.

The 360-interview is one of the most common approaches for a leader and an executive coach to uncover leaders' professional blind spots. Often, the executive coach will interview several stakeholders who work with the leader to identify attitudes and behaviors that either help or hinder the leader's performance. Rarely do all the interview insights qualify as blind spots. Most leaders are fully aware of their destructive behaviors but keep doing it anyway. However, occasionally the interviews reveal something surprising.

Instead of plowing through the entire themes report, I decided to share a brief anecdote summarizing my essential findings with everything I had learned from Vetter's stakeholders.

"What would you say is the one behavior holding Leah back from performing at her best?"

"She talks too much," said the stakeholder without hesitation.

"Interesting. What percentage of the time would you estimate she talks in a meeting today?"

He replied, "Fifty percent!"

"So, in a sixty-minute meeting with seven to eight other leaders and staff, the president is talking for thirty minutes of the time. Out of curiosity, what percentage of time should the president talk in a meeting?"

"Five percent!"

I could see the disappointment on Vetter's face when I shared the anecdote. She looked physically hurt by the story. Then her energy shifted. Her face and shoulders relaxed as she leaned back in her chair. She then said to herself aloud, "I have to stop proving my credibility and start building our credibility."

Vetter explained that even after a year in the role as president, she still felt insecure about her ability to do the job. It was easier for her to fall back into her old comfort zone of closing deals, especially in sales situations. She then began scribbling notes in her journal. I asked her what she was writing down.

She said with a hint of relief in her voice, "I have to let that version of me go. That's not my job anymore."

In his book *Team of Teams*, General Stanley McChrystal compares a leader's growth to the senior levels to a dinosaur's tail when he says, "As a leader grows more senior, his bulk and tail become huge, but like the brontosaurus, his brain remains modestly small." Vetter, the new president, was beginning to realize the size of her "dinosaur tail" and how her behavior was limiting everyone's performance.

It's been three years since I collected 360-feedback for Vetter. I reminded her of this moment in an interview and asked her what she learned from the experience. Here is what she had to say: *"Good intentions don't necessarily make you good at your job. I have learned that as a leader, my discomfort, coupled with my desire for winning, was the very thing preventing the team and me from developing the skills necessary to make us better."* Vetter used these insights to explore ways of showing up differently, modulated her approach, and redefined "winning" to be more inclusive.

This is the final chapter in this book. Up to this point, I've shared with you several strategies for behaving and thinking in ways to be more believable. When you avoid the behaviors that hurt your credibility and become more adaptable, you increase your believability. Let some fires burn and work on the system more, and you will elevate your believability even more.

Changing the way you lead and manage others will take your believability even further. It's on this level where you build trust not just in yourself, but also in your team. It's here you can maximize your impact and have the most significant influence on your organization as a leader. To complete the transformation, you must avoid being a bad manager.

THE FOUR HORSEMAN OF MANAGING PEOPLE
"I'm too busy."

"It would be easier to do it myself."

"My team doesn't have enough experience to do this on their own."

"I know what to do."

"I wish I could trust them."

"Failure is not an option."

If you've ever thought to yourself or said these words aloud, you might be a bad manager. This is overly simplified, but there are bad managers and good managers. Some of the bad managers are simply bad managers because they are bad people. You know who they are, and I'm willing to bet you're not one of them.

Some bad managers are good people but don't understand how their desire to be helpful and productive hurts their team. These behaviors are the most hurtful because they come from good people with good intentions. I call these bad behaviors born out of good intentions the Four Horseman of Managing People because they can spell doom for you and your team's believability.

The Four Horseman of Managing People may at first blush look innocent to you. They may even look like what a manager is supposed to do because you believe these behaviors are helping your team.

1. Leading from the Front
2. Instinctual Decision Making
3. Giving Advice
4. Solving Problems

At the core of these behaviors is a belief your team is an extension of your effectiveness, meaning it's their job to help you get things done. This flawed philosophy prioritizes work over people. It trades long-term value for short-term progress, even if that progress comes at the expense of the believability of your team.

FEEL	I want to be helpful	I want to move quickly	Don't enjoy seeing people struggle	I want to win
	✓	✓	✓	✓
DO	Give advice	Instinctual decision making	Solve the problem	Lead from the front
RESULT	Don't develop inner resourcefulness	Team doesn't understand the rationale behind decisions	Don't learn from mistakes	Tells team you don't trust them
DO INSTEAD	Ask questions	Explain how to think about problems	Allow the team to learn from experience	Use principles and concepts

An alternative and better approach is to expand your definition of winning to include leaving the work, team, and individuals better than you found them. This approach is working on the system and expanding your influence because it multiplies your ability to impact the organization. Your team will be more believable today and in the future.

The first approach is acting like a manager. The second is caring like a leader. To be more believable, you want to do the latter. The recommendations below address the Four Horseman of Managing People, what to watch out for, and what you should do instead.

LEADING FROM THE FRONT

John Plaso is senior vice president with Bellisio Foods and one of my former managers. His story began, as he told me in an interview, "in a factory working on the floor." Plaso has seen just about everything in there is to see in business. He has done everything from loading trucks at a Nestlé plant as a young business student to being the VPGM of billion-dollar brands. Plaso has all the experience and skills to lead from the front. What's interesting, and what makes John so good, is he leads from behind.

"The man on top of the mountain didn't just fall there" is a Vince Lombardi quote that could be taped to every manager's desk. Leaders like Plaso, who reach the middle and senior ranks, often have an incredible work ethic, a strong desire to win, and a track record of success to prove it. The paradox is to become a leader, you must have the desire and do the work required to win. But to be a leader, you must cultivate the desire and let others do the winning.

When a manager leads from the front, they are willing to do whatever it takes to win at the moment. Their desire to be helpful and productive leaves less room for their team to learn and grow. The manager remains in the spotlight and, by doing so, communicates they don't trust the team with the outcomes. It's what Vetter, from earlier in this chapter, was doing when she was doing most of the talking in meetings and trying to close the deals. She was putting her desire to win above growing the team's capabilities.

What was Plaso's secret? "I have a philosophy that you just surround yourself with the best people possible who think differently than you do," he told me in an interview over Zoom. I reminded him of something he did when he was my manager. It had a considerable influence on me, so I asked him to explain his methods.

I led the Banquet brand as a director while the VPGM role was open for over a year. Plaso took the VPGM role and, on the first day, pulled me aside and explained our new roles.

"I'm people and money. You are ideas."

He reflected on his statement, a message I've since learned he has shared with many of his employees. He explained, "If I get into the lower level of detail, I'm crowding middle management, and they're just going to take my ideas and go." He concluded, "I don't think I have the best ideas." He purposely stays out of the idea department to leave enough room for his team to grow into their roles. He was providing me space to grow, making it abundantly clear how I should invest my time.

He kept his word. He pushed me to develop a winning strategy that would transform our business yet stayed in his lane the entire time. He asked questions and challenged me to think bigger at every turn, but never offered up ideas. He created the space for me to be my best and surrounded me with all the talent and resources to succeed.

How do you lead from behind? Start by living by the rule "make your partner look good." It's a rule from improv, a creative theater game where the actors make up the stories and scenes on the spot in front of live audiences. It's hysterical and wildly entertaining to watch because of its free-flowing and spontaneous feel. It may appear unstructured, but improv has specific rules that make it work. One of those rules is to make your partner look good.

If your aim in every interaction is to make your team members look good, you can't fail. That's what John did. He didn't compete with us for the spotlight. He did the opposite by challenging us to develop ideas for maximizing and transforming our businesses. If we missed the mark on an assignment or presentation, he would coach us to be better next time. When we did something great, he would make sure we received all the credit. This is leading from behind, intentionally moving backstage so you can make everyone else look good.

INSTINCTUAL DECISION MAKING

If you can drive a car and talk simultaneously, you understand the fundamentals of instinctual decision-making. Once you've learned these skills, you no longer need to think about them consciously because they have become as natural for you as breathing.

A similar phenomenon takes place at work. When a person becomes a manager, they most likely have a ton of experience in the area, which means they can assess the situation and make decisions quickly and confidently. If you're a manager, then this is likely one of your strengths.

Unfortunately, the unintended consequence of your efficient decision-making is the team never learns the principles behind the decision-making process. They experience the result but remain unclear on how the results were achieved. They witness your outcomes but never learn the process themselves.

Suppose you find yourself needing to review the documents, presentations, and decisions of your team before they can be sent beyond your department. In that case, you have an opportunity to remove yourself from the process. It will be good for you because you already have too much to do each day. It will be good for your team because they need room to grow their capabilities.

There are two things to consider if you find yourself in this situation. First, you are prioritizing being right over getting better. You and the team successfully made it through this challenge, but the team didn't grow as much as it could from the experience. Second, you will be back here again to decide next time because your team didn't learn anything last time.

The challenge is often the decisions you are making feel urgent. Something or someone is waiting on this decision from you or your team, and they need it to be correct and done quickly. So, what do you do? You make the decision.

I learned this lesson the hard way. Each month I was responsible for forecasting the volume for my business. It involved lots of spreadsheets and analysis. The stakes were high for this activity because the manufacturing plant would produce millions of frozen dinners and pot pies based on my estimates. I didn't do this alone; there were many smart people helping me, but I was the person who took the heat when we were wrong.

My background in finance and analysis made me very competent in running the numbers on our forecast and explaining variances to plan. I could quickly assess and explain what was going on in the business just by looking at a page full of numbers. The problem was teaching other people how to do it well enough that I didn't need to be as involved in the process so I could work on the more strategic parts of the role.

The challenge for most managers and for myself is they are what Martin M. Broadwell described in his 1969 Gospel Guardian article as "unconsciously competent." Managers like these are good at what they do, but they can't articulate why they are good at what they do in a way that's helpful for others.

Instinctual decision-making by managers is making the decision but not helping others understand why you made a particular decision. It hurts the team's long-term ability to make decisions independently because they don't understand the thought process.

To overcome this challenge, you as the manager need to take a step back to what Broadwell calls the "Conscious Competent" level. You can objectively look at your thinking process and break it down to be more consumable for your team.

To make your decision process more transparent, you need to ask yourself three questions. These are the same three questions I ask myself when putting together any learning and development topics for the managers I train.

1. **What is the objective?**—This question makes you articulate what you're trying to achieve with the decision or teaching. It's explaining how you want to go about making the decision. It may be evident to you, but likely not to your team. State it clearly so anyone can understand it.

2. **What is the process?**—This question helps you think through the steps you naturally go through to make a decision. It can include what inputs you collect, what signs you're looking for, or how you reach your decision. This process probably happens pretty fast when you're doing it yourself. The goal here is to slow that process down and make it visible to others.

3. **What are the outcomes?** This question provides you the opportunity to explain your expectations. When you make a decision, you develop some sort of expectation. Defining the outcome, you hope to achieve with the decision. It's different from the objective because it describes the desired end state from making the decision. The objective focuses on how you want to make the decision.

The steps above helped me overcome my need to be at the center of the volume forecasting process. By asking the questions above, I learned my process was to ask myself a series of analysis questions in a particular order. My process helped me reveal potential mistakes in the volume forecasting. I made a list of those questions and shared them with the team.

Finally, I provided the team with my expectations for the forecast and how we would present it to senior management. Years later, I learned from my former employees the questions I provided to replicate my process are the same set of questions they shared with their employees. I was able to remove myself from the process, and they grew their abilities and passed them on to the next generation.

SOLVING PROBLEMS

Flight BA 5390, carrying eighty-one passengers, was headed from Birmingham, UK, to Malaga, Spain. When the aircraft reached 17,300 feet, the pilot's window separated from the plane, causing immediate decompression. The pilot, Tim Lancaster, was nearly sucked out of the opening, but luckily his feet became tangled with the controls long enough for someone to grab his legs.

In an interview for the Sydney Morning Herald, flight attendant Nigel Ogden described the scene and said, "I whipped around and saw the front windscreen had disappeared and Tim, the pilot, was going out through it—he had been sucked out of his seatbelt and all I could see were his legs." Ogden rushed to grab Lancaster around the waist and keep him from being fully sucked out of the window. At the same time, First Officer Alastair Atchison took emergency actions to save the airplane from a fatal nosedive.

With the pilot half out the window and extreme airflow in the cockpit making it hard to communicate with the ground, copilot Atchison was able to land the aircraft safely in South Hampton twenty minutes later. All souls on board, including Lancaster, landed safely. Lancaster survived the entire ordeal and returned to flying the same plane five months later.

Pop Quiz:
  1. What is the job of a pilot?
  2. What is the job of a flight instructor?

The pilot's job is to get the plane and its passengers to their intended destination safely. The job of the flight instructor is much different. The flight instructor's job is to create more pilots. They are responsible for helping their students develop the competence and confidence to become pilots.

Picture a student pilot and their flight instructor flying on a sunny afternoon. At the first sign of turbulence, the flight instructor takes control and does the flying for the rest of the lesson. How competent would the student pilot be if they never experienced any struggles?

Would you want to be a passenger in the plane of a pilot whose only lessons came from watching the instructor? Not on your life. You want a pilot who has experienced every possible scenario. If something happens on your flight, they know what to do and can do it quickly.

To fly as an airline pilot, the FAA requires fifteen hundred hours of flight time to earn an airline transportation pilot license. The reason for this is clear: the FAA wants to ensure the pilot has spent enough time in the pilot seat to know what to do should things go wrong.

Copilot Atchison had eleven hundred hours of experience flying the One-Eleven airplane. This extensive experience helped him know what to do to land the aircraft without the usual checklist or help from the air traffic control tower.

Perhaps not this exact scenario, but Atchison had trained for extreme conditions and had the experience necessary to do the job when called upon.

What Atchison demonstrated in those dire moments was resourcefulness. His actions proved he could find quick and clever ways to overcome difficulties in the face of danger. You reached your position as a manager because of your resourcefulness. You learned the hard way what to do when things go wrong. Resourcefulness is a competence that can't be taught with instruction alone. It's a combination of skill and confidence that comes from experience.

The challenge is it's hard to watch someone else struggle. It's the reason we have "helicopter" and "snowplow" parents. We don't want to see people we care about, or who work for us, fail, so we solve problems for them. When we jump in and solve problems, we are the flight instructors who grab the stick and take over. When you solve problems, the people around you take less initiative and can't earn their experience to become great pilots.

The solution is to allow your team to learn from their experiences. Even better, put them in challenging situations to struggle and learn more about their role and themselves. You don't have to allow them to fail, but you can give them more room to make mistakes. Never making mistakes isn't a realistic objective. You can't prevent all mistakes. But you can teach your employees how to recover quickly. It's what makes you a great pilot—your ability to solve problems quickly. You have an opportunity to be a great flight instructor by creating great pilots.

Adopting the flight instructor mentality will make you a more believable manager. From the copilot's seat, you can let them fly the plane as much as possible and only jump in to help if both of you are in imminent danger. The result is growth for them and you. They learn to be more resourceful, and you learn to multiply your influence and impact others by doing less.

GIVING ADVICE

Pam McClean, CEO of the Hudson Institute of Santa Barbara and a master coach, asked for a volunteer to join her in the center of the room to receive some coaching on a life challenge. There were twenty-five of us sitting in a giant circle in a meeting room at the Upham Hotel in Santa Barbara, California. Each of us was there to begin a year-long executive coaching training course.

Like many of my peers in the grand room, I came to the executive coaching program because I love helping people. There is nothing more exciting to me than helping someone with a challenge they face. I love to read books and share sage wisdom in the form of metaphors and advice.

Rick raised his hand to join Pam in the middle of the circle. He was sitting across from Pam and began presenting his problem while she listened intently. Within a minute or two, I had assessed the situation and developed several ideas to solve the problem.

I was surprised when Pam kept asking questions when the solution was so obvious. She dug deeper and deeper with her inquiry. Then suddenly Rick let out an "aha" and said, "It's so obvious now. I'm thinking about this all wrong." With only questions grounded in genuine curiosity, Pam helped Rick uncover a pattern in his life and illuminated an entirely new way forward.

It turns out I wasn't the only person surprised by what had just taken place. When asked about doing so little and being so helpful, the master coach responded with, "Your presence is the intervention." What she was teaching us was how we are more helpful when we do less.

Most managers believe their job is to dish out the work to their teams and then give employees advice on solving problems that arise. Until this experience, I thought the best way to be helpful was to share my hard-earned advice with others to make their jobs easier. Watching a master in action, I realized people don't want your solution. They want their solution.

Think about your friends and family for a moment. I'm sure many of them come to you with problems and ask for your sage advice. So, let me ask you something, and be honest. How often do they take your advice? I can say with certainty my advice is the absolute best available. (Seriously, I offer fantastic advice that is always spot-on!) But what I've noticed is how often that advice falls on deaf ears. People don't want your solution. They want their solution.

So now you might be thinking, "My team asks for my advice all the time, and they do what I tell them to do." Well, of course, they do; their paychecks depend on it. They also probably take a little less responsibility for their actions because you told them to do things in a certain way. That's managing the work, not leading the people.

So, am I suggesting never to offer advice? No, of course not. If someone is drowning, you should not ask them a question. Throw them a life preserver. Michael Bungay Stainer says it best in his book *The Advice Trap* when he wrote, "Stay curious a bit longer." Stainer is suggesting you lead with questions rather than advice.

Asking more questions and offering less advice will make you a better manager. You already know what you know. The advantage for you is you can learn what your staff knows by asking more questions. By asking questions, you get a glimpse into their thinking process. With this information, you can better assess their strengths and weaknesses. The advantage for your team is they learn to think critically about problems. Their new problem-solving competence will lead to a higher sense of autonomy and satisfaction.

~~~~~

There are bad managers, and there are good managers. Most bad managers are good people with good intentions. They earned their positions based on their experience and competence to do the work. Making the transition to being a good manager requires avoiding the Four Horseman of Managing People. It means setting all those strengths aside and putting your team's capabilities ahead of making progress. When you do this long enough, you not only build your believability, but you build their believability, too.

Conclusion

———

"You weren't put on the stage to be average," is something I remind myself when I am about to move to the front of the room or take the stage to influence others.

This pearl of wisdom was delivered to me at a keynote speaker training by a small-framed woman with short spiky hair. The class was about using movement to make our stories more engaging. She invited me to stand on the stage in front of the class and practice my presentation while using newly learned movements and gestures.

She told me to begin my keynote presentation and then stopped me almost immediately. As friendly as she could, she said, "Jeff, you seem like a really nice guy, but I need you to know something."

Her tone became more direct as she stated, "You weren't put on stage to be average." She explained it's natural to want to be humble and avoid drawing attention to ourselves as we go about our lives. However, the stage is the last place to be modest. The stage is for educating, entertaining, enrolling, and influencing the masses.

Looking directly into my eyes, she said, "I put you on the stage to perform!"

She turned to the class and said, "Write this down. It's a mistake to be average!"

~~~~~

Building your reputation with hard work and expertise leads to a reputation for dependability. These are great qualities to have, but they are not enough. Dependability is the same strategy everyone else is using which means it's a strategy for being average. Your work and career are your stage, and the worst thing you can do on it is to be average.

Believability will increase your influence and your impact on people exponentially. Treating how you do things with equal importance as what you do will give you the substance and style to differentiate yourself from the pack. Being more believable is anything but average and a requirement if you want to earn a seat at the table.

~~~~~

It's been fourteen years since that day in the pool where I learned I needed to change my strategy to swim like a swimmer instead of swimming like a runner. The paradigm shift helped me realize I also needed to adapt my strategy for influencing others at work. I needed to transform people's perceptions of me from being dependable to being believable.

On Thursday nights, I take my son to swim practice at that same pool. While there recently, I noticed something was written on the chalkboard for the collegiate swimmers.

"You can be anything you want in life. You just can't be everything you want in life. You must choose."

You can choose to be more believable at work.

Do you know what happens if you do? They will make room for you at the table because you have earned your seat.

Acknowledgments

Writing a book was way more challenging than I expected, and it couldn't have been done without lots of support and encouragement from some really amazing people.

The first person I need to thank is my lovely wife, Jen. She supported me through the entire writing process. She listened when I needed to vent my frustration. She encouraged me when I wanted to give up. She challenged me to see the big picture when I was thinking too small. She read every word of this book multiple times, even when it was a complete mess. In short, Jen made me feel loved, something she's been doing for as long as I can remember. Thank you for being my lobster. ROL.

A huge thank you goes to my business partner Nicole Bianchi, who declared one day, "We're going to write our first books this year," and then went and did it first so I wouldn't have any excuses. Nicole has paved the way for me in countless ways, and I couldn't imagine running a business or writing a book without her support and partnership. Nicole, you are the best!

Thanks to my children, Brady and Mallory, who tolerated my many mood swings while writing and editing this book. You gave me an "Okay, Francis" when I took myself too seriously, or a "You're the best around!" dance when I needed it most. I couldn't be prouder of you both. Swim fast. Have fun. No mercy!

To my parents and sister, Darrel, Robin, and Hailee, thank you so much for cheering me on and being the first people not to be surprised when I said I was writing a book. I appreciate all the love you have shared with me.

Thank you, Steve Kane and Zack Johnson, my *Ax and Yoke* brothers who started the journey with me. Knocking over those first dominos together directly led to writing this book. I appreciate all your support, and thank you for reminding me to chop wood and carry water when I didn't feel like touching the bar.

Thanks to Chad Samuelson and Brady Marlow for listening to my stories, helping me make them better, and telling me if they were book-worthy or not. Your friendship means the world to me.

Thank you, Sam Vetter, for always taking my chicken scratch ideas and making them better and more presentable to the world. Without you, I'm just a guy playing the tambourine.

I have had the good fortune to work with several brilliant leaders over my career. Many of them have graciously shared their wisdom with me, not just in interviews for this book, but also in life. This book and its ideas wouldn't be possible without Chris Dill, Derek Neeley, Steve Booker, Bill Nunez, Leah Vetter, John Plaso, Jennifer Baker, Krista McDonald, John Pawlowski, Gareth Miles, Chris Brocky, Sam Owens, Chris Routh, and Chris Alford. Thank you for all you have shared with me.

To all my campaign contributors: You pre-ordered this book before it was finished, which means you were betting on me, for which I am forever grateful. Your early orders made publishing this book possible and gave me confidence that I had a story worth telling. Thank you from the bottom of my heart.

Leah Vetter, Steve Kane, Greg Harris, Steve Booker, Robin Lasater, Abhijeet Saraf, Kristel Daly, Chad Samuelson, Brady Marlow, Nic bianchi, Taylor Dieckman, Amelis Long, Nicole Bianchi, Stacy Fuller, Dawn Dreessen, Melissa Tennison, Hannah Lefler, Christopher Dill, Joanne Stadnik, Ryan Hahn, Ashish Kothari, Nate Russell, Gary "The American," Shannon Dill, Laura Kapustka, John Pawlowski, Walter Sprang, Dave Koll, Michael Messerole, Darrel Shannon, Kate Briganti Weaver, Bart Hendryx, Curtis Stowe, Jordan Adams, John Saunders, Katie Arbataitis, Steve Getzfrid, Anne Biernacki, Steve Clawson, Jon Finnegan, Matt Dunn, Paul Scolan, Beau Baumert, Jason Geolingo, Susan Henricks, Matthew Stejskal, Kelly Schaefer, Josh Kahrs, Patrick Ricketts, Wade Horst, Ziyuan Yang, Jocelyn Carley-Wynn, Jisella Dolan, Jina Paul, John Plaso, Kevin Weber, Dave Bianchi, Christiane Brocky, Jen Wulf, Melissa Stigge, Nicole Serena, Ricky Anderson Jr, Matt Giese, Heidi Couch, Jennifer Mulholland, Duane Maciejewski, Robert McCutcheon, Benjamin Beckham, Deanna Vansickel, Aamna Farooq, Erin Condon,

William Nunez, Burke Wilson, Nerissa Morris, Nathan Penney, Frieda Herron, Sheri Wells-Chesley, Chris Routh, Paul Scholz, Bill Hahn, Luke Paladino, Tracy Wilk, Brandan Kitt, Carolina Migliaccio, Brett Gay, Carrie Molczyk, Eva Roberts, Taylor Williams, Eric Koester, Matt Kresl, David Marzahl, Kyle Perry, Shane Miller, Amy Patterson, Rachelle Hood, Annamarie Mann, Jeffrey Korengel, Kurt Campman, Jen Egan, Scott Cunning, Carole Sprunk, Matthew Dugan, Christi Annin, Alejandro Castro, Ben Reynolds, Joe Trouba, Jeanne Jones, Brandi Ballan, Krystal Stubbendeck, Joe Rupp, Zack Johnson, Steve Gale, Kelly Straus, Sakthi Prashanth, Mosah Goodman, Monica Vogel, Michael Novak, Lonnie Snyder, Chef Avenue, Joey Patterson, Scott Bowen, John Vyhlidal, Chris Alford, Tim L'Heureux, Daniel Nash, Crystal Zamora, Robby Renshaw, Alexis Knight, Katherine Porto, Michaela Blocklinger, Samantha Bristol, Amy Grafelman, Oluwaseun Olaore, Devon Torskey, Kimberly McCants, BaiLeigh Leach, Kimberly Vasquez-Rosete, Jasmyn Flowers, Kirsten Placzek, Yajaira Gonzalez, Christopher Walker, Michael Chapman, Kendra Wright, Kayla Sommer, Chelsey Goodwin, Paul Ternes, Alex Sass, Elizabeth Sawhney, Yuki Weinberg, Abranda Andersen, Frank Rozmus, Katina Granger, Nicole Overkamp, Alli Greene, Karah Thompson, Maria Jimenez, and Mark Moulton.

Thank you to Caroyln Chamberlin and the Special Olympics staff, board members, volunteers, and athletes for teaching me so much about life, love, and competition. A portion of the pre-sale campaign proceeds went to SONE to further transform people's lives in Nebraska with and without disabilities through programming in sports, health, and education.

Thank you to Eric Koester and the Creator Institute! Eric, your energy and enthusiasm are unmatched, and without you none of this would be possible. Thank you for building a program that makes writing a book not only doable but enjoyable, too!

To Quinn Karrenbauer—Most of your recommended improvements were spot-on. Thanks for challenging me to be a better writer. Sorry I was so resistant to your early feedback!

A big thank you to the publishing team at New Degree Press, who held my hand through the entire process: Brian Bies, Kathy Wood, Linda Berardelli, Jordana Megonigal, and Amanda Brown.

Appendix

―――

INTRODUCTION

"About TI Technique." Accessed May 11, 2021. http://www.totalimmersion.net/about-ti-technique.

Inc, Gallup. "What Is Job Quality? The Full Story of Great Jobs." Gallup.com. Accessed May 11, 2021. https://www.gallup.com/analytics/318188/great-jobs-success-story.aspx.

"Simon Sinek Inc. on LinkedIn: There's No Such Thing as 'Soft Skills' | 3119 Comments." Accessed May 11, 2021. https://www.linkedin.com/posts/simon-sinek_theres-no-such-thing-as-soft-skills-activity-6785052836100100096-hJxi.

CHAPTER 1

GO FURTHER UPSTREAM

"A Global Survey on the Ambiguous State of Employee Trust." Harvard Business Review, July 22, 2016. https://hbr.org/2016/07/a-global-survey-on-the-ambiguous-state-of-employee-trust.

Brown, Fleur. "How to Build Your Personal Brand without the *Cringe*." Medium, April 24, 2020. https://medium.com/your-brand/how-to-build-your-personal-brand-without-the-cringe-25ff154e36d3.

Collider. "The 30 Highest Grossing Actors of All Time, Ranked," July 3, 2019. https://collider.com/galleries/most-profitable-highest-grossing-actors/.

Handwerk, Brian. "45,000-Year-Old Pig Painting in Indonesia May Be Oldest Known Animal Art." Smithsonian Magazine. Accessed May 11, 2021. https://www.smithsonianmag.com/articles/45000-year-old-pig-painting-indonesia-may-be-oldest-known-animal-art-180976748/.

Henry, Todd. Herding Tigers: Be the Leader That Creative People Need. New York: Portfolio, 2018.

IMDb. "Malice (1993)." Accessed June 17, 2021. https://www.imdb.com/title/tt0107497/.

Influencer Marketing Hub. "What Is Personal Branding [Free Personal Brand Health Checker]," September 10, 2018. https://influencermarketinghub.com/what-is-personal-branding/.

July 29, Sarah Lynch Published: and 2019. "Taylor Swift's Former Manager Shares Career Advice on His Podcast // ONE37pm." Accessed May 11, 2021. https://www.one37pm.com/culture/music/rick-barker-taylor-swift-blueprint-interview.

"Limbic System: Amygdala (Section 4, Chapter 6) Neuroscience Online: An Electronic Textbook for the Neurosciences |

Department of Neurobiology and Anatomy—The University of Texas Medical School at Houston." Accessed May 11, 2021. https://nba.uth.tmc.edu/neuroscience/m/s4/chapter06.html.

"Looking Back: LeBron James' 10 Trips to The Finals | NBA.Com." Accessed May 11, 2021. https://www.nba.com/lebron-james-past-finals-trips-history.

Marketplace. "Dany Garcia Is One of the Most Influential People You've Never Heard Of." Accessed May 11, 2021. https://www.marketplace.org/shows/corner-office-from-marketplace/dany-garcia-is-one-of-the-most-influential-people-youve-probably-never-heard-of.

MJD. "Taylor Swift Albums and Songs Sales as of 2021." Chart-Masters (blog), May 25, 2021. https://chartmasters.org/2021/05/taylor-swift-albums-and-songs-sales/.

Press, Eric Olsen Associated. "Deserted Icons: No College World Series Hits Omaha Hard." Press Herald (blog), April 11, 2020. https://www.pressherald.com/2020/04/11/deserted-icons-no-college-world-series-hits-omaha-hard/.

Rory Vaden Official Site. "Take the Stairs Book by Rory Vaden | New York Times Bestselling Author." Accessed May 11, 2021. https://www.roryvaden.com/take-the-stairs.

Statista. "Most Influential People on Twitter 2020." Accessed May 11, 2021. https://www.statista.com/statistics/1100266/top-influential-twitter-users/.

"The Stories Behind 10 Famous Product Placements," April 6, 2008. https://www.mentalfloss.com/article/18383/stories-behind-10-famous-product-placements.

Trinh, Stories by. "3 Reasons Why You Should Cultivate a Kick-Ass Personal Brand." Medium, May 1, 2020. https://medium.com/your-brand/3-reasons-why-you-should-cultivate-a-kick-ass-personal-brand-40c4dc22e80.

UA Newsroom. "Project Rock Through The Work." Accessed May 11, 2021. https://about.underarmour.com/news/2020/02/project-rock-through-work.

CHAPTER 2

DON'T GIVE AWAY YOUR POWER

Berker, Archy O. de, Robb B. Rutledge, Christoph Mathys, Louise Marshall, Gemma F. Cross, Raymond J. Dolan, and Sven Bestmann. "Computations of Uncertainty Mediate Acute Stress Responses in Humans." Nature Communications 7, no. 1 (March 29, 2016): 10996. https://doi.org/10.1038/ncomms10996.

Coach John Wooden. "Motivational Quotes." Accessed May 11, 2021. https://www.thewoodeneffect.com/motivational-quotes/.

Divine, Mark. Unbeatable Mind: Forge Resiliency and Mental Toughness to Succeed at an Elite Level. 2nd edition. CreateSpace Independent Publishing Platform, 2014.

Farnam Street. "How to Use Occam's Razor Without Getting Cut," October 28, 2019. https://fs.blog/2019/10/occams-razor/.

"Five Hindrances—Ajahn Brahm." Accessed May 11, 2021. https://www.budsas.org/ebud/ebmed051.htm.

"How to Survive in the 'Digital Amnesia' World." Accessed May 11, 2021. https://usa.kaspersky.com/blog/digital-amnesia-survival/5548/.

Khan Academy. "What Is Power? (Article) | Work and Energy." Accessed May 11, 2021. https://www.khanacademy.org/science/physics/work-and-energy/work-and-energy-tutorial/a/what-is-power.

Master Shi Heng Yi—5 Hindrances to Self-Mastery | Shi Heng YI | TEDxVitosha. Accessed May 11, 2021. https://www.youtube.com/watch?v=4-079YIasck.

ScienceDaily. "New Theory of Synapse Formation in the Brain." Accessed May 11, 2021. https://www.sciencedaily.com/releases/2013/10/131010205325.htm.

SHAWSTRENGTH. "Bio." Accessed May 11, 2021. http://shaw-strength.com/bio/.

Trevor Moawad Discusses His New Book "It Takes What It Takes" On Cheddar TV. Accessed May 11, 2021. https://www.youtube.com/watch?v=-Jj1rl7zGfA.

"The Strangest Secret." Accessed May 11, 2021. https://www.nightingale.com/articles/the-strangest-secret/.

"Will Bowen—YouTube." Accessed May 11, 2021. https://www.youtube.com/user/awillbob.

CHAPTER 3

DRINK THE ANTS

1 Big Virtual Event Idea That Changes Everything! Accessed May 16, 2021. https://www.youtube.com/watch?v=gp1_nYOaCd8.

An Invention without a Future. Accessed May 16, 2021. https://www.ucpress.edu/book/9780520279742/an-invention-without-a-future.

CrossFit Alinea. "What Is CrossFit?" Accessed May 16, 2021. https://www.crossfitalinea.com/what-is-crossfit.

Daily Stoic. "Remember: You Don't Control What Happens, You Control How You Respond," March 13, 2020. https://dailystoic.com/remember-you-dont-control-what-happens-you-control-how-you-respond/.

Holiday, Ryan. Stillness Is the Key. New York: Portfolio, 2019.

https://kurzweilai.net. "The Law of Accelerating Returns « Kurzweil." Accessed May 16, 2021. https://www.kurzweilai.net/the-law-of-accelerating-returns.

LLC, CrossFit. "CrossFit: Preparing for the Unknown and Unknowable." Accessed May 16, 2021. https://games.crossfit.com/video/crossfit-preparing-unknown-and-unknowable/games.

Mingis, April Montgomery, and Ken. "The Evolution of Apple's iPhone." Computerworld, October 15, 2020. https://www.computerworld.com/article/2604020/the-evolution-of-apples-iphone.html.

Morning Chalk Up. "What Fraser and Medeiros Discussed During the Long Run Back," October 25, 2020. https://morningchalkup.com/2020/10/24/what-fraser-and-medeiros-discussed-during-the-long-run-back/.

Nead, Nate. "Media and Entertainment Industry Overview." InvestmentBank.Com (blog), February 11, 2018. https://investmentbank.com/media-and-entertainment-industry-overview/.

Pruitt, Sarah. "The Lumière Brothers, Pioneers of Cinema." HISTORY. Accessed May 16, 2021. https://www.history.com/news/the-lumiere-brothers-pioneers-of-cinema.

"Table 1. Median Years of Tenure with Current Employer for Employed Wage and Salary Workers by Age and Sex, Selected Years, 2010-2020." Accessed May 16, 2021. https://www.bls.gov/news.release/tenure.t01.htm.

The Liar. "101 Zen Stories: A Cup of Tea," June 28, 2020. https://itstheliar.wordpress.com/2020/06/28/101-zen-stories-a-cup-of-tea/.

CHAPTER 4

LET SOME FIRES BURN

Clason, George S. The Richest Man In Babylon: The Success Secrets of the Ancients—the Most Inspiring Book on Wealth Ever Written. New York, NY: Signet, 1988

Clifford, Catherine. "Bill Gates Took Solo 'think Weeks' in a Cabin in the Woods—Why It's a Great Strategy." CNBC, July 28, 2019. https://www.cnbc.com/2019/07/26/bill-gates-took-solo-think-weeks-in-a-cabin-in-the-woods.html.

Co-op, R.E.I. "REI Co-Op Publishes 2019 Full-Year Financial Results." REI Co-op, April 27, 2020. https://www.rei.com/newsroom/article/rei-co-op-publishes-2019-full-year-financial-results.

Inc, Gallup. "Work and Workplace." Gallup.com, September 6, 2007. https://news.gallup.com/poll/1720/Work-Work-Place.aspx.

JOURNAL, Robert A. Guth Staff Reporter of THE WALL STREET. "In Secret Hideaway, Bill Gates Ponders Microsoft's Future." Wall Street Journal, March 28, 2005, sec. News. https://www.wsj.com/articles/SB111196625830690477.

Masters of Scale. "Selina Tobaccowala on Masters of Scale." Accessed May 21, 2021. https://mastersofscale.com/selina-tobaccowala-let-fires-burn/.

"REI Co-Op Continues #OptOutside Tradition, Closing on Thanksgiving and Black Friday." REI Co-op. Accessed May 21, 2021. https://www.prnewswire.com/news-releases/rei-co-op-continues-optoutside-tradition-closing-on-thanksgiving-and-black-friday-301143774.html.

Statista. "Retail Sales Growth Forecast 2022." Accessed May 21, 2021. https://www.statista.com/statistics/232347/forecast-of-global-retail-sales-growth/.

CHAPTER 5

ACT LIKE AN OWNER

"2019 United States Small Business Economic Profile." US Small Business Administration—Office of Advocacy. Accessed May 29, 2021. https://cdn.advocacy.sba.gov/wp-content/uploads/2019/04/23142719/2019-Small-Business-Profiles-US.pdf.

BrainyQuote. "F. Scott Fitzgerald Quotes." Accessed May 29, 2021. https://www.brainyquote.com/quotes/f_scott_fitzgerald_100572.

Brandon, Emily. "How Much to Contribute to a 401(k)." How Much Should You Contribute to a 401(k)? (blog), December 7, 2021. https://money.usnews.com/money/retirement/401ks/articles/how-much-should-you-contribute-to-a-401-k.

Carrier. "Carrier History | Carrier Air Conditioning, Heating and Refrigeration." Accessed May 26, 2021. https://www.carrier.com/carrier/en/worldwide/about/history/.

Entrepreneur. "Sam Walton," October 9, 2008. https://www.entrepreneur.com/article/197560.

Hayes, Thomas C. "Sam Walton Is Dead At 74; the Founder Of Wal-Mart Stores." The New York Times, April 6, 1992, sec. US https://www.nytimes.com/1992/04/06/us/sam-walton-is-dead-at-74-the-founder-of-wal-mart-stores.html.

Kennedy, Michael. "Sam Walton: A Legacy of Customer Obsession." Medium, February 8, 2017. https://michaelkennedy999.

medium.com/sam-walton-an-enduring-example-of-customer-obsession-a197b4446a53.

McIntyre, Georgia. "What Percentage of Small Businesses Fail?" Accessed May 29, 2021. https://www.fundera.com/blog/what-percentage-of-small-businesses-fail.

Nolan, Quinn. "Sam Walton Got Arrested." Medium, October 15, 2019. https://medium.com/@quinnnolan/sam-walton-got-arrested-67c3534496f6.

"Table 7. Survival of Private Sector Establishments by Opening Year." US Bureau of Labor Statistics. Accessed May 29, 2021. https://www.bls.gov/bdm/us_age_naics_00_table7.txt.

WNYC Studios. "How the Air Conditioner Changed America | The Takeaway." Accessed May 29, 2021. https://www.wnycstudios.org/podcasts/takeaway/segments/how-air-conditioner-paved-way-ronald-reagan.

CHAPTER 6

NEVER SKIP LEG DAY

"A Survival Guide for Leaders." Harvard Business Review, June 1, 2002. https://hbr.org/2002/06/a-survival-guide-for-leaders.

College of Engineering—Purdue University. "System of Systems." Accessed May 30, 2021. https://engineering.purdue.edu/Engr/Research/Initiatives/Archive/SoS.

Dec 08 and 2020. "How Many Flights Per Day? Airline and Flight Statistics (2021)." Gay Travel, December 8, 2020. https://www.gaytravel.com/gay-blog/airline-and-flight-statistics.

Executive Forum. "Cutting Off the Ends of the Ham," February 10, 2017. https://www.executiveforum.com/cutting-off-the-ends-of-the-ham/.

Flight Literacy. "Aircraft Systems," November 29, 2017. https://www.flightliteracy.com/aeronautical-knowledge/aircraft-systems/.

Masters of Scale. "Brian Chesky on Masters of Scale." Accessed May 23, 2021. https://mastersofscale.com/brian-chesky-hand-crafted/.

Peter Skillman Design. "Peter Skillman Design." Accessed May 23, 2021. http://www.peterskillmandesign.com.

Peter Skillman Marshmallow Design Challenge. Accessed May 23, 2021. https://www.youtube.com/watch?v=1p5sBzMtB3Q.

Ranker. "How Long It Would Take You To Travel From New York To California Throughout American History." Accessed May 31, 2021. https://www.ranker.com/list/cross-country-travel-in-american-history/bailey-benningfield.

"Seven Transformations of Leadership." Harvard Business Review, April 1, 2005. https://hbr.org/2005/04/seven-transformations-of-leadership.

CHAPTER 7

BECOME THE MOUNTAIN CLIMBER

"14ers.Com • Online Guidebook." Accessed June 1, 2021. https://www.14ers.com/routes.php.

Derr, Alex. "How Many Fourteeners Are In Colorado: 53 or 58? There's No Easy Answer." The Next Summit (blog), October 18, 2020. https://www.alexmderr.com/how-many-fourteeners-are-in-colorado/.

Dweck, Carol S. Mindset: The New Psychology of Success, 2007.

Indiana Jones and the Last Crusade (1989)—IMDb. Accessed June 1, 2021. http://www.imdb.com/title/tt0097576/characters/nm0248848.

Institute For Altitude Medicine. "Physiology." Accessed June 1, 2021. http://www.altitudemedicine.org/physiology.

"Like Magic? ('Every System Is Perfectly Designed…')." Accessed May 23, 2021. http://www.ihi.org/communities/blogs/origin-of-every-system-is-perfectly-designed-quote.

Payne, Matt. "100summits—Colorado&#39's 12 Hardest 14ers to Climb." Accessed June 1, 2021. http://www.100summits.com/articles/mountaineering-tips/item/258-colorados-12-hardest-14ers-to-climb.

Popova, Maria. "Fixed vs. Growth: The Two Basic Mindsets That Shape Our Lives." Brain Pickings (blog), January 29, 2014.

https://www.brainpickings.org/2014/01/29/carol-dweck-mind-set/.

Satel, Sally. "The God Committee." The God Committee (blog), June 17, 2008. https://www.aei.org/articles/the-god-committee/.

Sedaris, David. "Laugh, Kookaburra." The New Yorker. Accessed May 31, 2021. https://www.newyorker.com/magazine/2009/08/24/laugh-kookaburra.

"Special Olympics Nebraska: Home." Accessed June 6, 2021. https://www.sone.org/.

The Broadmoor Manitou & Pikes Peak Cog Railway. "The Broadmoor Manitou & Pikes Peak Cog Railway." Accessed June 1, 2021. https://www.cograilway.com/.

"The Seattle 'God Committee': A Cautionary Tale | Health Affairs Blog." Accessed May 31, 2021. https://www.healthaffairs.org/do/10.1377/hblog20091130.002998/full/.

CHAPTER 8

SEE LIKE THE HUMMINGBIRD

"Discovering the Electromagnetic Spectrum." Accessed June 17, 2021. https://imagine.gsfc.nasa.gov/science/toolbox/history_multiwavelength1.html.

Hotz, Robert Lee. "Different Wavelengths: Science Finds Hummingbirds See Ultraviolet Light Invisible to Humans."

Kansas City Magazine. "This Small Town Kansas Photography Shop Develops Aged Film Formats No Other Processor Will Touch," December 7, 2020. https://www.kansascitymag.com/dwaynes-photo/.

"Kodachrome (2017)—IMDb." Accessed June 2, 2021. https://www.imdb.com/title/tt1880399/.

Riel, Jennifer, and Roger L. Martin. Creating Great Choices: A Leader's Guide to Integrative Thinking. Boston, Massachusetts: Harvard Business Review Press, 2017.

Stoddard, Mary Caswell, Harold N. Eyster, Benedict G. Hogan, Dylan H. Morris, Edward R. Soucy, and David W. Inouye. "Wild Hummingbirds Discriminate Nonspectral Colors." Proceedings of the National Academy of Sciences117, no. 26 (June 30, 2020): 15112–22. https://doi.org/10.1073/pnas.1919377117.

Sulzberger, A. G. "For Kodachrome Fans, Road Ends at Photo Lab in Kansas." The New York Times, December 30, 2010, sec. US https://www.nytimes.com/2010/12/30/us/30film.html.

CHAPTER 9

F.O.C.U.S. ON DECISIONS

Annie Duke. "How To Make The Right Decisions Even When You Don't Have All The Facts," August 15, 2018. https://www.annieduke.com/how-to-make-the-right-decisions-even-when-you-dont-have-all-the-facts/.

Duke, Annie. Thinking in Bets: Making Smarter Decisions When You Don't Have All the Facts, 2019.

Gawande, Atul. The Checklist Manifesto: How to Get Things Right. 1st edition. New York, NY: Picador, 2010.

George, Alison. "Can You Tell a False Memory From a True One?" Slate Magazine, September 8, 2013. https://slate.com/technology/2013/09/eliza- beth-Loftus-interview-false-memory-research-on-eyewitnesses-child-abuse- recovered-memories.html.

Heath, Chip, and Dan Heath. Decisive: How to Make Better Choices in Life and Work, 2013.

IMDb. "Argo (2012)." Accessed June 17, 2021. https://www.imdb.com/title/tt1024648/.

CHAPTER 10

GET OUT OF THE WAY

"A Quote by Vince Lombardi Jr." Accessed June 12, 2021. https://www.goodreads.com/quotes/19425-the-man-on-top-of-the-mountain-didn-t-fall-there.

Beall, Taylor. "Today in Aviation: British Airways 5390." Airways Magazine (blog), June 10, 2021. https://airwaysmag.com/today-in-aviation/british-airways-5390/.

"Conscious Competence Learning Model." Accessed June 12, 2021. https://www.businessballs.com/self-awareness/conscious-competence-learning-model/#origins.

Condé Nast Traveller India. "Mayday! Incredible Stories of Pilots Who Saved the Day," June 28, 2016. https://www.cntraveller.in/story/mayday-incredible-stories-of-pilots-who-saved-the-day/.

"How Long to Become a Pilot / ATP Flight School." Accessed June 12, 2021. https://atpflightschool.com/become-a-pilot/airline-career/how-long-to-become-a-pilot.html.

McChrystal, Stanley Gen, Tantum Collins, David Silverman, and Chris Fussell. Team of Teams: New Rules of Engagement for a Complex World, 2015.

NZ Herald. "Image of Pilot Hanging out Window Captures Heroic Story 30 Years On." Accessed June 12, 2021. https://www.nzherald.co.nz/travel/image-of-pilot-hanging-out-window-captures-heroic-story-30-years-on/GR2HBBCBUGMOTA-7MEYPI7UR54A/.

Stanier, Michael Bungay. The Advice Trap: Be Humble, Stay Curious & Change the Way You Lead Forever. Page Two, 2020.